The Bridesmaid's Manual

The Bridesmaid's Manual

Make it To and Through the Wedding with
Your Sanity (and Your Friendship) Intact

SARAH STEIN AND LUCY TALBOT

BERKLEY BOOKS, NEW YORK

THE BERKLEY PUBLISHING GROUP
Published by the Penguin Group
Penguin Group (USA) Inc.
375 Hudson Street, New York, New York 10014, USA

USA I Canada I UK I Ireland I Australia I New Zealand I India I South Africa I China

Penguin Books Ltd., Registered Offices: 80 Strand, London WC2R 0RL, England
For more information about the Penguin Group, visit penguin.com.

This book is an original publication of The Berkley Publishing Group.

Library of Congress Cataloging-in-Publication Data

Stein, Sarah.
The bridesmaid's manual : make it to and through the wedding with your sanity
(and your friendship) intact / Sarah Stein and Lucy Talbot.
pages cm
ISBN 978-0-425-26436-2
1. Bridesmaids.   2. Wedding etiquette.   3. Weddings—Planning.   4. Female friendship.
I. Title.
BJ2065. W43S745   2013   2013009615
395.2'2—dc23

PUBLISHING HISTORY
Berkley trade paperback edition / August 2013

PRINTED IN THE UNITED STATES OF AMERICA

10 9 8 7 6 5 4 3 2 1

Cover design: Diana Kolsky and Emily Albert.
Cover image of Wedding Cupcakes copyright © Ruth Black / Shutterstock.
Text design by Laura K. Corless.

SARAH'S DEDICATION:

For Isabel, Olivia, and Ben

LUCY'S DEDICATION:

To the memory of Gordon Kato,
trusted friend, agent, and advisor

ACKNOWLEDGMENTS

I would like to acknowledge all of the brave and beleaguered bridesmaids who shared their wedding party stories with us. We recognize you did so not with revenge in your heart (okay . . . maybe a little revenge . . .) but with intent to help (and potentially save) those future bridesmaids who would walk down the aisle after you. To you, we are most grateful. I would like to thank Ilana Stern, founder and CEO of weddingtonway.com, for sharing her wedding style expertise; Daniel McFadden, makeup artist to the stars and artistic genius, who shared his beauty knowledge; and finally, Allyson Levine, of Bob Gail Events in Los Angeles, for sharing some of the latest party planning ideas. I would also like to thank the following brides—Alison, Debbie, Ilene, Stephanie, Risa, Jodi, Wendy, and Stephanie again—upon whose weddings I cut my first bridesmaid teeth, and my very wonderful and supportive boyfriend, Scott, with whom I've agreed to elope one day. And finally, I would like to thank my agent, Elisabeth Weed, for her constant encouragement (and occasional kick in the taffeta pants) and our amazingly talented, unbelievably energetic, and incredibly patient editor, Andie Avila.   —*Sarah Stein*

I'd like to express my thanks and appreciation to our sharp-eyed and savvy editor Andie Avila, and to all the brides and bridesmaids who shared their colorful stories with us.   —*Lucy Talbot*

TABLE OF CONTENTS

Table of Contents

INTRODUCTION

Congratulations! He popped the question, she said yes, and then she popped the question, and you said yes.

If you've opened this book, it's likely that you have been chosen—nay, handpicked—by a close friend or relative who is a beaming bride-to-be to perform the sacred duties of bridesmaid. You are most likely filled with excitement because you will get to stand by one of your favorite people in the world on her most important day. And you are somewhat filled with trepidation, as you will devote months, if not the year ahead, to making sure that the big day and the important events surrounding it meet her every expectation. And at this point you are probably thinking, *Uh, now what?*

You may feel unsure of what to do or where to begin, or you may be wondering why you even accepted the job in the first place—you agreed hastily, out of love, admiration, and gratitude. Or maybe you said yes out of a sense of obligation only because she felt close enough to you to ask you. (When was the last time you even spoke to this person?) You are probably confused and possibly a little regretful—you've heard horror stories from friends and are aware that you'll be committing your time, energy, and a good portion of your hard-earned savings to someone else's romantic venture.

Here's the deal: It's a big honor, but it's also a big job. Not so long ago, a bridesmaid could pretty much assume she would meet a few times with fellow bridesmaids to plan a bridal shower and attend a traditional, "normal" house-of-worship wedding. She would be dressed from head to toe in pastel organza and would modestly celebrate at the reception before tossing handfuls of rice and other nonbiodegradable goods at the departing happy couple. No longer. In the past fifteen years, since our first book, *The Bridesmaid's Guerrilla Handbook*, was published, weddings and wedding planning have changed dramatically. And with that, so, too, has the role of a bridesmaid changed.

You'll have to negotiate plans for showers, a bachelorette party (possibly out of town), luncheons and dress-shopping sessions (Kleinfeld, here we come!) with a bunch of women with wildly conflicting schedules and with whom you have very little in common (including style and taste) other than a relationship with the bride-to-be. You'll also be expected to wear, say, and do things that you'd probably rather not wear, say, or do. You'll also have to play therapist—listening and devoting attention to the bride as needed. These duties may come at inconvenient times, such as in the middle of the workday when the bride will call to discuss the arcane minutiae of bridal fairy-tale land—vacillating between a birdcage or blusher lace veil she found on Etsy—while your boss is standing at your cubicle. You may wonder, *When did a magic wand turn a bridesmaid into the bride's personal serf?* Could it have anything to do with the first big royal wedding, the "wedding of the century" that 750 million people tuned in to watch in 1981 when Charles, Prince of Wales, married the demure young Lady Diana Spencer on a perfect summer day? Even women who did not view the original have seen rebroadcasts, and the pomp and ceremony of that fairy-tale wedding is dazzling to behold. And of course, Kate Middleton's wedding to Prince William reignited the flame of our collective imagination; fairy-tale weddings can come true, one could happen to *you*. And if it doesn't, well, you can always just re-create your own at your local country club. Or so think the thousands of brides who catch Royal Wedding Fever. But to pull off that level of splendor and spectacle takes a lot of loyal retainers. Or very dedicated bridesmaids.

While being a bridesmaid is a labor of love, don't be fooled— it's still hard labor. The job will test your mental strength, your emotional fortitude, and the limits of your savings account. But here's the good news. We're here to help guide you on this journey—escorting the bride from the rowdy halls of singlehood to the threshold of marital bliss—so that it's less arduous and you're more at ease in your newfound role.

Be aware that no matter how strong your ties with the bride may be, the engagement period is a time of heightened emotions in a bride's life and therefore in yours as well. Many relationships have been cemented and severed over the bride's perception and expectations of a bridesmaid's fulfillment of her responsibilities. Now is not the time to falter as a supportive friend. Instead, now is the time to set aside your own preferences, disgruntled rumblings of "You're making me wear what?!" and thoughts of hog-tying the bride with Tiffany Blue ribbon and leaving her on the reformer of a Pilates studio. Now is the time to step up to the plate and gird yourself for the enormous task at hand. Because your time will come. Or maybe it already has and she was there for you. Come to think of it, you do *kind of* owe her for making her herd an angry swan away from that lakeside cocktail reception.

It's quite possible that you're thinking, *Okay, I get it. This is a huge time in the bride's life. But how long is my tour of duty, er, this engagement, going to last? Six months? A year? MORE?! How long do I really need to make my friend's life my priority?* Well, whatever the length of the engagement, there's certainly no question that it will feel as though you'll be at someone else's beck and call a really, *really* long time. It's no wonder that during this period, the friendship might feel a little one-sided—the most common of bridesmaids' complaints. After all, you can only be *so* interested in hearing about the bride's tussles with her mother over the guest list or the cheapness of her future in-laws that spells doom for her rehearsal dinner.

In defense of these brides, they are just really excited. It's like they've been waiting their whole lives for someone to "put a ring on it," and, naturally, they want their day, week, or year to savor it, celebrate, and enjoy feeling special. The wedding industry is fueled (and funded) by this very idea—that your wedding is the pinnacle of your life, and every detail needs to be absolutely perfect to ensure the future happiness of the bride and groom. Even the most levelheaded bride learns the hard way that once you start planning a wedding, it takes on a life of its own. We're not making excuses; we just want to point out that even the strongest and most sensible women may fall victim to the belief that this time in their life, and every detail involved, is as fascinating and important to everyone else as it is to them. It can feel all-encompassing to the bride, and she'll be leaning on you for support!

And maybe now you're thinking, *Oh no! I can't do this. I just want to go to a couple of parties. I'm happy to help plan a shower, but I definitely don't want to hear about this wedding every day for the next year!* Well, maybe you won't have to. Many brides are quite reasonable. And if things get out of control, as a friend, you always have the right to say to the bride that you'd like to go a night without any wedding talk. The truth is, she's just so thrilled to have found her better half and have you be a part of this special time in her life. And it's possible that's all she's thinking about. And if she's thinking about it, she's going to want to talk to you, her best friend, about it. And if you agree to talk about it, she's going to want you to understand that she *needs* real monarch butterflies as place cards. And once you've realized your previously rational friend's sanity is missing in action, you'll have to feign interest until you can slip away to answer that booty-call text you just got. "Oh, no! My grandma Flo needs me to help her change her catheter. Gotta go!"

Once you've agreed to sign on as a bridesmaid and perform the task and all it entails (and we know you have, otherwise you wouldn't be reading this book), you're in for the duration. Even if you are dealing with a Bridezilla who has lost sight of the fact that asking someone to be her bridesmaid is not just an honor but a *favor*, you don't have the right to refuse to purchase your dress and to spend the entire wedding reception telling tales of the bride's sexual conquests during college.

It is so important for your well-being that you recognize your commitment and simply accept that, as a bridesmaid, there are responsibilities and a code of conduct you are expected to follow. Regardless of your feelings about wearing a pumpkin-hued gown for a Halloween wedding, when you say yes, you are signing on the dotted line. You have made a pact with the bride, and you agree to provide the services of bridesmaid during her engagement and through the wedding reception. It is your job do everything you can (within reason, of course) to help make this time wonderful and something special to remember.

We're not here to sugarcoat—we're here to help. Help you help the bride; help you help your fellow bridesmaids; help you maintain your sanity . . . if not your dignity. But how is this honesty going to prove helpful to you in the months ahead? Well, we're not just going to speak the truth; we'll give you answers to all those pesky questions: What do I pay for? What do I say when another bridesmaid tries to force her bad taste upon the group or suggests a really awful idea? When can I ask the bride if I can bring a plus one? We'll provide you with ideas, tips, and advice for all that budgeting and planning you'll have to do. And we'll share useful tips and tools from the experts (beauty specialists, wedding planners, *and* real women who have been in your dyeable shoes before).

The self-respecting bridesmaid needs to be prepared, equipped, and ready to launch into action. Why be passive when you can be proactive? This handbook will be indispensable to you throughout the bride's engagement period. Everything you'll ever want to know about being a bridesmaid is now at your fingertips. Keep it on your night table and carry it in your handbag; download it onto your tablet or your phone, which will inevitably ring or vibrate around the clock till the wedding is over.

But don't worry about being on call. We'll tell you what you can expect, clearly outline your responsibilities as a bridesmaid, and show you where to draw the line! Our hope is to see you glide through your duties, maintain your sanity, and keep your friendship intact. We expect that by the time you've finished reading this book, you'll learn how to remain upbeat through the less-than-fun parts and appreciate all the great moments that emerge during this time. With knowledge and preparation, you'll sail through months of planning and partying with confidence and savvy, enjoying the journey and savoring the day when all your efforts help make the bride shine. And who knows, maybe that usher escorting you down the aisle won't be so bad after all.

1

Will You Be My Bridesmaid?

You always knew this day would come—ever since since your best friend from preschool plopped the long white veil from the dress-up box on her own little head and handed you the crushed silk flower wreath, demanding you "hold her train." Her announcement was filled with excitement, anticipation, and expectation, especially when she asked you to be her bridesmaid.

Filled with emotion, your reply was simply: "What an honor! I'd love to be your bridesmaid!" At the time, you didn't think too much about what that entailed, but now that a few hours, days, or weeks have passed, you're wondering where to begin. And you may even be feeling a little unclear on what you've gotten yourself into. Let's start by explaining the origins of the tradition.

Contrary to most people's beliefs, the bridesmaid's place in the wedding ceremony extends beyond leading a wedding march down the aisle and serving as decorative filler in photos. And we don't mean holding the bride's dress up as she maneuvers into a tiny bathroom stall to pee. Bridesmaids actually serve an extremely useful and critical function in the wedding ceremony and throughout the engagement period leading up to it.

As far back as the ancient Greeks, the bridesmaid's place in the ceremony was celebrated for the joy and happiness she contributed to the event. In the days of antiquity, most women were married by the time they turned sixteen. The first bridesmaids were a group of older married women (wrinkly old crones of around twenty-four years old) who escorted the young, inexperienced bride to the wedding as well as accompanied her throughout the marriage process. Since just about everything served some symbolic purpose to the Greeks, it was believed that if fertile, happily married women accompanied the young bride, their good fortune would extend to her. This entourage was also believed to stave off evil spirits until the marriage ceremony was completed.

In Anglo-Saxon times, it was considered unmaidenly for a bride to enter marriage willingly, and it was common practice for prospective brides to be "captured" by future husbands. Hence, it was necessary (if only for maintaining appearances) for a bride to gather her friends to protect her from this possibility. Oh no! The men are coming! These early bridesmaids helped fend off inappropriate (and unwanted) suitors (not entirely unlike a clique of middle school girls). Or, if the bride was on board with the match, the maids assisted the groom's efforts in whatever way possible while still maintaining the façade of unwillingness. Conversely, the best man was always a friend of the groom who helped him capture the object of his affections. In those days of reaping and sowing, it was possible that said lady would have a brother (or five) the size of a linebacker, and it was necessary for a marriage-minded man to choose the "best" man for the job. Hence, the earliest best men were often broad-shouldered and muscular (not exactly bad news for those bridesmaids). Nowadays restraining orders are pretty easy to procure, so not as many brides need help fleeing from a determined suitor.

For years, weddings remained in the realm of traditional. A man and a woman got engaged. The woman and her mother invited hundreds of people to a ceremony at their country club, yacht club, catering hall, and maybe, if they were bohemians, a cornfield in Woodstock. But, like everything else in our globalized world, weddings and wedding-attendant duties have evolved. The modern bridesmaid needs to know more. From the hottest trends to the latest technology that will allow her to execute perfect plans while watching an episode of *Downton Abbey*, the modern bridesmaid needs to be prepared for the unusual and unexpected.

Today's Bridesmaid

Because the function of a bridesmaid has changed so dramatically over the centuries, it is necessary to redefine her duties as they pertain to the realities of today's society. If you're lucky, you'll still have to fend off hot young men at the reception, but your new official task is to perform a range of services and functions that will assist the bride through the modern marriage process. You're a member of her crisis-management team, her advisory council, and her social committee. She'll cry on your shoulder, call upon (then disregard) your good taste when making decisions about color schemes and flower arrangements, and expect you to dance with her sweaty-palmed brother at the reception. But you love her. And because you said yes and gladly accepted the honor, you have to honor her requests. As a maid of honor or bridesmaid, you can't say no—not without major repercussions. Be aware that it is the rare bride who realizes just how much she is asking of a friend or relative. (If you fancy yourself a rebel, go directly to Chapter 12, "Just Say No!")

The bridesmaid is an emotional ballast, a troubleshooter, and a hostess. The wedding ceremony and related festivities include significant investment, financially and emotionally. Ideally, the resulting memories will justify the necessary expenditure and the inevitable accompanying stress. While spending money on travel, the bridesmaid dress, the engagement party dress, matching shoes and accessories, and gifts is unavoidable, knowing in advance exactly what is expected of you and what expenses are headed your way will help reduce your stress. It's also not a bad idea to find out as soon as possible who your sisters-in-arms will be—before you agree to dress like them, coordinate schedules with them, and make them your bosom buddies over the next six months to a year.

Performing as a bridesmaid is a daunting task not to be taken lightly. If you're the kind of person who has never been good at

Do you know why bridesmaids and ushers dress alike (preferably similar to the bride and groom)? It's supposed to confuse any evil spirits intent on harming the bride and groom. The tradition evolved because wedding processions in Europe used to run from the bride's home through the village. Dressing alike ensured that if the wedding party ran into a jilted ex, he wouldn't know upon whom to put the whammy.

taking a backseat to anyone, acceptance of this post may involve an attitude check. However, the payoff can be enormously rewarding. You're an honored guest with a crucial role in one of the most important days in a close friend's or family member's life, and you'll see that beyond planning a shower, listening to a litany of wedding troubles and bitch sessions about the future mother-in-law (FMIL), the most useful service you can provide for the bride is simply that of a really, really good friend.

If you are completely surprised that the bride has asked you to be a bridesmaid—perhaps it's been several years since you've seen each other—you may, after considering the invitation, decide you feel uncomfortable renewing your acquaintance through a commitment that requires so much time and energy. Ask the bride how involved she expects you to be in the process. Some have an entire

The Cast and Crew

So There's You, but Who Are the Other Players?

Bride

Groom

Mother of the Bride (MOB)

Father of the Bride (FOB)

Sister of the Bride (SOB)

Brother of the Bride (BOB)

Future Mother-in-law (FMIL)

Future Father-in-law (FFIL)

Future Sister-in-law (FSIL)

Future Brother-in-law (FBIL)

Maid of Honor (MOH)

Bridesmaids

Flower Girl

Ring Bearer

Best Man (BM)

Wedding Planner (WP)

support group of local family who help with the nuts and bolts of the wedding planning and only want their bridesmaids to show up on time and participate in the ceremony. It could just be her way of reaching out to a cherished friend and a lovely way to renew the friendship. Life pulls us all in different directions, but sometimes when we are lucky, it brings us back together with the people who have brought warmth and joy to our lives along the way.

Now that we've discussed the tradition and covered general expectations, let's move on to the nitty-gritty.

2

Where to Begin

You've graciously accepted the invitation to be a bridesmaid, and in doing so, have made a vow to the bride-to-be. You've promised to be an active and willing participant in her wedding ritual. That's right, we said *ritual*. Yes, you're talking about a one-day event, but there's a process involved here. You've agreed to assist the bride throughout the duration of her engagement period. The one little issue is that you're clueless about what to do next.

Knowledge is power, though, and here you'll learn all that is expected of you. You'll get a handle on the bridesmaid's responsibilities and duties, and you'll be able to figure out a starting point.

Responsibilities and Duties

The important thing to remember is that in every wedding there are customary duties of the attendants, and then there are the bride's interpretations and preferences, which can be anything but customary.

A bride should not assume that her bridesmaids know exactly what is expected of them, and her bridesmaids should never hesitate to say "Um . . . I have no idea what the h°ll I'm supposed to do! A little guidance, please." Of course, don't actually say it like that. And if you have said this, that's probably why you ended up with a copy of this book.

One way modern brides are bridging this gap of expectations is by writing welcome notes to their bridesmaids. The letter outlines the bride's general plans for the engagement period—whether or not you'll be helping with any additional or untraditional costs and the events you're expected to attend. Some brides take this too far, presenting their bridesmaids with what is more akin to a list of demands.

If the bride has not sent out welcome letters, there are acceptable questions to ask and a right way to ask them, such as, What color will the bridesmaid dresses be? Are you going to have an engagement party? And then there are those questions one shouldn't ask, to which the savvy attendant should already know the answers. If you're asking, Can I have your Amex number so I can buy my dress? or Can I start drinking in the receiving line? and these questions don't seem inappropriate to you, read on and take notes.

Customarily, the Bridesmaid:

- Offers to assist the bride in any reasonable way with wedding plans.

• Offers to accompany the bride to any wedding-dress shopping and fittings.

• Offers to run errands leading up to the day and on the day of. This might mean jumping in your rental car on the morning of the wedding and programming your GPS to head to an airport an hour and a half away to pick up the bride's favorite aunt whose plane was rerouted there.

• Makes herself available for bridesmaid-dress shopping.

• Attends all pre-wedding parties and related events.

• Helps the maid or matron of honor plan the bridal shower and provides the equitable financial contribution (see Chapter 7, "The Bridal Shower").

• Records all gifts and their respective givers at the bridal shower (note: only one or two bridesmaids need to do this). Tucks this list away where the bride can find it so she can properly thank friends and family for their generosity.

• Offers opinion on designs for wedding website, save the dates, wedding invitations, and the like. In the olden days, when people didn't have computers and they wrote by candlelight, they needed bridesmaids to help avoid the writer's cramp inevitable in hand-addressing five hundred envelopes. Today, people use their own printers or hire a calligrapher, but you may be called upon to offer your opinion on designs. Honesty is always the best policy, but follow the Golden Rule and carefully choose your words, especially if you are dealing with a sensitive bride.

- Functions as a cohostess at the wedding and pre-wedding festivities. This does not mean you have to offer to freshen everyone's drinks and chat with each guest. However, it does mean you should be an active participant at the events. After all, you are the wedding "party." Think of yourself as part of the popular crowd, at least with regard to wedding functions. You have a responsibility to be friendly to the other guests— both those you know and those whom you haven't yet met— and dance. If the guests see you having fun, they'll want to get in on the fun, too.

- Pays for her own bridesmaid dress, shoes, and accessories. And a bridesmaid never considers purchasing or wearing shoes or accessories that she hasn't run by the bride. There could be a certain look or consistency the bride is striving for. And let us be the first to tell you that it may not appear to make one tiny bit of difference if you're wearing a shoe unlike that of the girl in the same dress next to you, but it really stands out in photos. Which, as we know, last forever.

- Pays for her own hairstyling and makeup. And again, photos do last forever. If you don't wake up looking naturally perfect, you may need a bit of professional help. If you live in the same town as where the wedding is taking place, you probably already have someone you can trust and rely on to help make you look your best. But the bride might want all of you to get ready together, in which case, be prepared to put yourself in the hands of someone new. And if the wedding is held out of town, you'll definitely be dealing with someone you've never met. Regardless of where you get pretty and with whose assistance, be clear that unless the bride specifically offers to pay your primping costs, this expense will come out of your own pocket.

• Is prepared to arrange for her own transportation to and from the ceremony and the reception, unless the bride has made specific arrangements for the attendants ahead of time. It's often helpful to carpool with the other bridesmaids. Just make sure you have a designated driver lined up or an alternative mode of transportation. Preorder a taxi or car to pick you up and take you home so you can drink without worrying about getting home safely.

• Pays for her own accommodations. These days, no matter if guests are traveling from near or far, brides will reserve a block of rooms for them well in advance of the wedding, and many brides prefer to keep the bridal party together. So before you book a room, check in with the bride or look on her wedding website to see if there's a particular place she'd like you to stay. If the place the bride has selected is outside of your budget, ask her tactfully for other suggestions.

- Precedes the bride in the processional. See Chapter 10, "At the Wedding!"

- Helps the maid of honor with the bride's bustle. If the MOH is all thumbs, it's likely this duty will fall on your shoulders. Be prepared, it can get kinda tricky back there. You'd think there are just a few hooks and eyes, but instead, you're confronted with some kind of strange origami-like beast. Find out ahead of time if the maid of honor needs your assistance, then you can attend one of the bride's dress fittings and have a saleswoman or seamstress at the salon show you how to do it.

- Greet guests in the receiving line. If there are more than fifty guests at the wedding, the bridal party will be expected to form a receiving line to meet and greet them. The maid of honor stands after the groom, and the bridesmaids are beside her. After the first half hour, bridesmaids may be excused from the line to go drink—we mean celebrate—while the bride, groom, and respective mothers continue to stand in the line. (See Chapter 10, "At the Wedding!")

- Dances with her designated usher at the end of the newly-weds' first dance. So what if the usher who escorted you down the aisle is five feet four and you're six feet tall. When the music begins and the bandleader or DJ calls you to the floor, you're there with a smile on your face and a spring in your step.

- Participates in the bouquet toss. This, of course, is the most torturous and demeaning of all wedding rituals. It implies that single women will do just about anything to catch a man, and that's just not a very modern perspective. However, if the bride wants to toss her bouquet to a group of maidens, it's your job to be there with your hands waving frantically in the air. You can always pretend to drop it if it comes your way or fumble it into the hands of a more enthusiastic recipient.

Plan of Action

A good way to dispel your anxiety about your role is to take some control by asking the bride questions that help you better understand her expectations and plan your own calendar and budget. Explain to the bride that you understand she is the star, the director, and the producer of her wedding, but as a member of the supporting cast, you need a copy of the script and the shooting schedule.

You can ask your questions in such a way that you establish parameters and subtly remind the bride that you have a life and responsibilities apart from her wedding project. A bride is thinking about many things when starting her planning process, but finding her dress is one of her main priorities that will likely involve you. If you want to help her get the ball rolling, or if you want to find out where she is in her plans, start by asking her questions about the dress. Here are some helpful examples to get started:

You: "Do you want any help wedding-dress shopping?" or "How soon will you want to start the dress hunt? I'm free these weekends." *TIP: Suggest four possible dates so she realizes you won't be at her beck and call for a dozen weekends.*

Bride: I don't know. It depends on which weekends Adam and I are testing menus or scouting out possible venues.

You: Okay, let me know once you narrow it down so I can be sure to join you. It would be a shame if I couldn't get out of another obligation, because I would like to help you shop for the dress. Unless it's easier for you to go with just your maid of honor?

This way you've let the bride know that if she requests your help at the last minute, you may not be able to accompany her.

If the bride tells you she already has appointments to visit a dozen department stores, boutiques, and wedding salons, ask her to e-mail you a list of the appointment times. Figure out what is feasible with your schedule and feels reasonable to you. An afternoon at Vera Wang may be fun, but all day at Kleinfeld could push you over the edge. If a schedule conflict exists, be up front about it. "I'd like to join you, but that day I have another commitment." And offer another time and day that works for you. You'll want to do the same when it comes to discussing the bridesmaids' dresses, which should happen as soon as she's found her gown.

The Bridesmaid's Budget

At the risk of repeating ourselves, weddings aren't cheap, so it shouldn't come as a surprise that being part of one isn't going to be inexpensive. If you want to fully participate in all of the pre-wedding events and festivities and aren't a trust-fund baby, you're going to need to do some serious financial planning if you don't want to appear, well, cheap.

In addition to paying for your dress, your shoes, and required additional accessories, you can expect to incur significant "hidden" expenses, such as transportation to and from the wedding, accommodations during the wedding (likely more than one night if you're participating in the rehearsal), and your share of the bridal-shower budget, the bachelorette party, and respective gifts. The average wedding can cost a bridesmaid anywhere between $600 and $2,000 before the bride and groom even say "I do." And while certain expenditures can't be avoided, with a little careful planning and strict budgeting, you'll still have enough money left over to pay the rent.

To help you plan your budget, turn the page for a worksheet with a list of fixed expenses you can expect as a bridesmaid. Enter the cost of each item (including the optional little extras), and create a budget so you know where all your hard-earned money is going. This process can help you save for that well-earned spa day you're going to need so desperately when it's all over.

Expense	Item	Estimated Cost	Actual Cost
OUTFIT	Dress		
	Shoes		
	Stockings		
	Bra/bustier/shape wear		
	Clutch/bag		
	New underwear*		
	Headpiece (hat, fascinator, etc.)		
	Alterations		
	Accessories: necklace, earrings, gloves, additional bling, double-sided tape		
Outfit Subtotal			
GROOMING	Hairdo		
	Haircut*		
	Hair color*		
	Facial*		
	Professional makeup		
	Waxing (facial and body)*		
	Manicure/pedicure*		
Grooming Subtotal			
TRAVEL	Airfare to/from wedding		
	Hotel/accommodations		
	Car to/from rehearsal dinner		
	Car to/from wedding		

Expense	Item	Estimated Cost	Actual Cost
	Tips for porters/maids/etc.		
Travel Subtotal			
BRIDAL SHOWER	Use worksheet in Chapter 7	Insert total here	
Bridal Shower Subtotal			
BACHELORETTE PARTY	Use worksheet in Chapter 8	Insert total here	
Bachelorette Party Subtotal			
GIFTS	Engagement		
	Bridal shower		
	Wedding		
	Baby (for shotgun weddings)		
Gift Subtotal			
BRIDESMAID'S TOOLKIT	Everything you'll need for the big day!		
THERAPY	Six visits with HMO therapist		
	A year of psychoanalysis		
	Therapeutic spa day		
	Shoe shopping . . .		
	Piece of jewelry to memorialize your service and survival; your "Purple Heart"		
Therapy Subtotal			
GRAND TOTAL			

Additional Expense: This is a potential, but discretionary, expense.

The Money-Saving Bridesmaid

There are significant expenses ahead, but you shouldn't feel as though you'll need to take out a loan for each and every one. If you strategize and consider some of the following ideas, who knows, maybe you'll even save enough to extend that oh-so-needed post-wedding spa day into a whole weekend of R&R!

• Look for Groupons or coupons for haircuts, hair coloring, and body waxes in advance of the wedding.

• Most bridal salons give a discount on the bridesmaids' dresses if the bride purchases her wedding gown at their shop. Ask the bride to inquire about this when she shops for her gown.

• If the bride chooses bridesmaids' dresses that are off-the-rack, consider websites like weddingbee.com and eBay, where former bridesmaids may be looking to unload/sell their A-line dresses in that perfect shade of honeydew. These sites are often cheaper than bridal boutiques and can offer a *wide* variety of dresses. One we love? Weddingtonway.com often has clearance sections, and again, if the bride is receptive, it's a great way to find an inexpensive dress.

• If the bride asks you to pick out your own dress, there are great sites that have wedding-appropriate dresses: erin fetherston.com, shopbop.com, jcrew.com, and revolveclothing

.com. Sign up for e-mail alerts so you'll know when there are sales, particularly Friends and Family sales at places like Bloomingdale's and Macy's. *TIP: Ebay.com and weddingbee .com can be great places to find dresses, but don't expect to find a number of dresses in the right sizes. Other good flash-sale sites to troll—gilt.com and hautelook.com. You can find really great deals on really great dresses. Just make sure you unsubscribe after you find your dress, or you could become addicted. Next thing you know, you're clicking your refresh button every five seconds around 9 a.m. waiting for the Marc Jacobs sale to start so you can be the first to nab that cute beaded purple top that would look so great with your black AG jeans. Just sayin' . . . it's a problem for some people.*

- If given the option to find your own dress, consider borrowing or renting one. Yes, renting. For a fraction of the cost of purchasing a dress, these services offer the opportunity to borrow a beautiful (and typically overpriced) dress for the evening. Renttherunway.com is a great place to start. When you're done, just send it back. Only one snag: If it gets stained, you're stuck with it. You can also consider sample sales. Call the showrooms of designers located in your city. Ask to be put on a mailing list for their sample sales.

- If you need a hotel room and want to cut down on the expense, consider sharing with another bridesmaid or out-of-town guest.

- If the bride isn't insisting on everyone getting their makeup and hair done by professionals for the wedding, consider doing your own. Totally challenged when it comes to beautification? YouTube.com has thousands of really great how-to videos for creating fabulous updos and elaborate makeup. Just practice before the big day. More than once.

- Traveling for the wedding? Check out Kayak, Expedia, Travelocity, and other online travel sites for the best hotel and airfare deals. You can also sign up for notifications on these sites to alert you to changes in fares to your destination city so you know you're getting the best price possible. Almost all hotels, B-and-Bs, and chains take reservations online, and most will offer a lowest-price guarantee or even a discount—if you book online.

- Hit a consignment shop to find great shoes on the cheap. There are so many shops with beautiful silk shoes that have never been worn or are barely worn. Consignment no longer means dirty clothes that smell like mothballs. Previously worn clothes and shoes in perfect and often unworn condition are easy to find. Or check out zappos.com, 6pm.com or weddingbee.com for shoes that beat retail price.

3

The Maid of Honor

One of the greatest honors any woman can bestow upon another is that of maid of honor at her wedding. By conferring this most sacred mantle upon you, the bride is acknowledging to the whole world that above *all* of her other friends, she's known you a little bit longer, she likes you a little bit more, and she loves you like a sister . . . or, of course, you are her sister. Either way, you have been given an important role in your friend's (or sister's) special day, and it's not a task to be taken lightly. And as much of an honor as it is to be asked, it is also a huge responsibility. You will be rallying the troops, leading the call to action, and if necessary, throwing yourself on live grenades to save the bride-to-be. The sweetest of friendships have turned sour over poorly performed maid-of-honor duties, and accepting the honor means you are embracing a host of responsibilities that put you in the eye of the storm—and require you to weather it.

Why You Are So Darn Special

The maid of honor (MOH), otherwise known as the honor attendant, is the premier bridesmaid, the leader, captain of the cheer squad. She is second-in-command only to the bride's mother and is required for even the most modest wedding ceremony, if only to serve as a legal witness. Usually a close girlfriend or relative, she is the bride's right hand, an assistant wedding coordinator, her confidante and consultant. In short, the maid of honor gets to boss around the other bridesmaids (and they can't do a thing about it)!

There are actually two kinds of honor attendants: the maid of honor and the matron of honor. While essentially they are the same, the first title refers to a woman who is single and historically, well, virginal, while the matron of honor refers to a woman who is married and (hopefully) not a virgin. The job description is the same, but tradition dictates this distinction (1) so the best man will know if he can cop a feel during the first dance, and (2) so the women at the ceremony can point and murmur, "What a shame—always a bridesmaid, never a bride." Some brides who are sticklers for protocol might ask, "Does this mean my maid of honor has to be a virgin?" No. If maids of honor had to be virgins, you'd be hard-pressed to find somebody to fit the bill. Especially if you're over twenty-five. The job would cease to exist. Luckily, modern society allows us this slight blurring of terminology so the maid of honor may walk down the aisle confident she won't be stripped of her title because she's living in sin with a drummer of an indie band.

If you are the maid or matron of honor, the bride will lean most heavily on you throughout her engagement and during the wedding reception. You'll be her emotional—and sometimes physical—ballast (many a bride has been known to get a little wobbly at the altar). You should be prepared to lend a helping hand from the moment you accept the position. The bride can't decide between the lavender chiffon gown with the matching shawl or the lemon tulle and bonnet getup? You're there. The bride wants to save money and tie ribbons around each napkin at every place setting (there are 400 guests) rather than have the caterer do it? You're there. The bride's ex shows up at her house despite the restraining order, and you're not there? Okay, but you *are* on the phone calling 911.

Sometimes a bride chooses to have both a maid and a matron of honor. This can be a convenient loophole for brides who are close with two women and don't want to pick favorites. Especially if one is married and the other is single. Today, it's not uncommon to have two maids of honor or two matrons of honor. And we say, why not? While traditional formal etiquette dictates that this is a no-no, today's weddings are far from ordinary, mixing tradition with personal preference in a way that truly reflects the individual tastes and personalities of the bride and groom. And if that bride and groom want to honor two friends with the same post? We say go for it. Besides, planning a wedding is stressful enough for a bride without her having to choose between two sisters or two friends to fill the position. The truth of the matter is that nobody has ever felt slighted for having to share the title of maid or matron of honor. The importance of the title is not diminished because you're sharing the post. However, two should be the max. If the bride has three or more sisters or friends of equal closeness and just can't choose one, perhaps you can suggest she make them bridesmaids and ask a special relative or friend to stand in as the honor attendant. It's just not chic for a group of women to crowd a groom at the altar. And you'll look more like an angry posse there to ensure the groom doesn't try to skip out.

What Am I Supposed to Do Again?

While it's a bridesmaid's responsibility to take an active role in all pre-wedding and wedding-day festivities, it is the MOH who is in charge of making and executing many of those plans. Her standard duties include all of the previously mentioned bridesmaid's duties as well as the following:

- **Compile wedding party contact list and send out pre-wedding newsletter.** Help the bride find a memorable way to notify her guests to save the date. (One bride mailed the details on paper snowflakes for a winter wedding.)

- **Escort the bride on any and all reasonable wedding-related errands.** No, you don't have to fly from San Jose to Portland, Maine, to view some obscure designer's wedding-dress designs, but if you live in the same city or town, you should set aside a mutually convenient time to go with the bride on basic errands like gown shopping, bridesmaid-gown shopping, choosing invitations, favors, meeting with wedding planner, et cetera.

- **Initiate plans for the bridal shower and act as party coordinator.** See Chapter 7, "The Bridal Shower."

- **Assist with any mailings.** Offer to help address wedding invitations. Luckily, with almost all wedding invitations these days being addressed by a professional calligrapher or printed with a computer program at home, the modern MOH is no longer expected to suffer writer's cramp in the name of love. However, this was once an expectation. Now the responsibility is more about assembling invitations (with RSVP cards, hotel information, and any other inserts the bride has ordered) and stuffing envelopes. Unfortunately, there is no machine as of yet that can do that, but we're waiting. Now that the United States Postal Service allows custom-designed stamps, the MOH might help the bride choose a tasteful personal photo that suits the theme of the wedding rather than the limited choices available at the local post office. On a recent afternoon, our post office had Mother Theresa, Garfield the Cat, and Dennis the Menace stamps available.

- **Choose the gift that the bridesmaids give the bride, and collect the money for it.** This additional gift is optional! Repeat—OPTIONAL! Most bridesmaids aren't even aware that there *is* an additional gift. Hey, maybe the bride won't know either. Feel free to use your best judgment with regard to this extra expense.

- **Coordinate the fittings for the bridesmaids' gowns.** The MOH should make sure that the bride has communicated to her bridesmaids exactly what she wants regarding hair, makeup, shoes, and jewelry. And make sure the bridesmaids understand the bride's vision for her bridesmaids' look.

- **Hold the bride's bouquet and her own during the ceremony.**

- **Hold the groom's ring during the ceremony.** Yes, with two bouquets in hand already, it's a lot to carry. Try putting it on your pointer finger before the service begins. Or maybe just try to convince the couple how great it would be to use their dog as a ring bearer.

- **Serve as a witness, both ceremonial and legal.** The MOH is a crucial witness in the wedding ceremony, even if the wedding is officiated by an Elvis impersonator in Las Vegas. Although the MOH traditionally signs the marriage certificate, the bride may choose another person to serve as her legal witness on other documents (such as the ketubah in the Jewish religion) in order to allow another friend or family member to play an honored role in the wedding.

- **Straighten the bride's train and veil after the processional, before the recessional, and during the photo shoot.** Any fashionista will tell you, "Don't neglect the rear view." How you look from the back is every bit as important as how you look from the front, and it's your job to police the bride's rear view so that even though she is facing away from her guests, she is sheer perfection. (Likewise, don't neglect your own rear view. Keep static cling and tucked hemlines in check before you march down that aisle.)

- **If you are the bride's sister and the bride is wearing a blusher, it is traditional that you lift her veil for the husband's kiss.**

- **Stand in the receiving line.** If the wedding is larger than fifty people, there will be a receiving line. (See Chapter 10, "At the Wedding!") Shake hands, smile, and be friendly. Yes, even to that nasty sorority sister who tried to sabotage your friendship with the bride in college.

- **Propose a toast during the reception.** This is optional—which may be music to your ears since many people are more afraid of public speaking than death. However, if you thrive in the spotlight, this can be a great opportunity to express your good wishes and "share the love" for the happy couple. It's a good idea to stay relatively sober until after you've given your speech. Sure, a glass of wine or shot of vodka beforehand can help calm nerves (we call it a cup of courage), but no one wants to listen to you blather on for twenty minutes about how much you love each and every person at the wedding. Have no idea how to lead a toast? We've provided you with a few speech starters in Chapter 10.

- **Assist the bride's mother in helping the bride change from her wedding gown into her going-away clothes.** This will also include helping the mother of the bride put the bride's dress away, not as easy as it sounds when puffy tulle presents a challenge. Just be glad you don't have to store it at your house. They don't yet make space bags for bridal gowns.

While the aforementioned tasks represent the most traditional duties performed by the maid of honor, there are other functions you can perform that are equally as indispensable to the bride. After all, as the maid of honor, you get to wear lots of hats.

- **Lady-in-Waiting.** A major duty for the role is bustling the bride's train. Pippa Middleton didn't have to worry about this task when sister Kate walked down the aisle of Westminster Abbey to marry Prince William. While the Duchess of Cambridge's train was nothing compared to the twenty-five-foot train worn by her late mother-in-law, Princess Diana, in 1981, the Duchess Kate actually changed into a different floor-length gown for her reception. However, most brides wear the same gown to the ceremony and the following reception, and it's your job to reconfigure the parking lot on her booty

The record for longest bridal train in history is 1.85 miles. The dress was designed by the Romanian fashion house Andree Salon. It took ten seamstresses nearly a hundred days to create.

into the appropriate taffeta origami sensation, that is, the bustle. There are lots of different kinds of bustles, but basically your task is to hook up the train in the back of the dress so that the hem lies evenly all the way around. The saleswoman at the bridal store, or the tailor, can show you how it's done. We suggest a trial run before the big day.

- **Team Leader:** This unlikely group of comrades is under your command, and they'll be looking to you for the 411 on everything wedding-related: "Who, what, where?" A great way to organize the group and make sure you're all on the same page is to set up an e-mail contact group or even a private group on Facebook. Set up the contact list so you are sure to send all e-mails to everyone. Don't get a response? Call. Many a plan has been ruined thanks to the disappearance of important e-mails falling into junk-mail folders. WARNING: A pitfall of e-mail is that tricky Reply All button. If one bridesmaid sends you an e-mail complaining about another bridesmaid or an idea, do *not* write back about what a pain that chick is; in your haste you could easily click Reply All rather than Reply. And it's just a good practice not to say anything you wouldn't want said about you. Likewise, be sure to check *all* e-mail threads you send out to be sure no private messages are included.

- **Make sure that the whole wedding party has one another's cell phone numbers and e-mail addresses.** This way, they can contact one another directly with any small (or personal) issues not worthy of your time.

- **To get the ball rolling, send a pre-wedding e-mail or news-letter to bridesmaids.** There are many templates on the Internet. You can use the same one every time and maybe send out a monthly update to the bridesmaids. Use the newsletter to remind the team about where they'll be having their hair and makeup done or where to meet for pre-wedding photos. Send reminders about scuffing up the bottoms of their new shoes for added traction and confirming/coordinating trans-portation to and from wedding-related events. An electronic newsletter is a great way to inform the whole party of impor-tant changes in plans and/or scheduled call times to ensure that everyone shows and there are fewer slipups. Want to avoid any electronic snafus? Use snail mail.

- **Head of Protocol.** It's 6:30 p.m. and guests are anxiously twitching in their seats—do you know where the rabbi is?

Make sure you do. As the assistant wedding coordinator, it's crucial that you have a copy of the bride's contact list with all the names and numbers of vendors, officiants, planners, musicians, beauticians, et cetera. An organized bride will have a group contact list on her computer that she can export and e-mail to you. Put that list in your phone. Have a less tech-savvy bride or you'd rather have a hard copy you can carry in your bag? Create a contact sheet with the names and numbers for all wedding attendants and service providers, such as the hairdresser and makeup artist.

- **Good Witch.** If the bride is superstitious, she may put you in charge of making sure the groom doesn't see her in her wedding gown before the ceremony begins; it's bad luck. You should know about these mysterious things. Another example? If the groom steps on the bride's gown or veil at the altar, he will dominate the household. If the bride steps on the tails of his coat, she'll control their home. (Maybe that's why tails don't touch the ground?) The maid of honor or the mother of the bride may drape the bride's veil over the groom's feet, dictating that the bride will control the home. The savvy best man will know to protect his buddy's controlling share and remove the veil, throwing it back to ensure the man will rule. Lucky for us, most men are clueless.

- **Double Checker.** The bride should have a checklist of all the things she'll need on her wedding day (dress, shoes, something old, something new). A day before the wedding, run through her checklist with her to make sure she has everything (and still have a day to pick up anything she doesn't have). Then run through it again on the day of the wedding before she leaves her house.

- **The Heavy.** While the bride and groom are the final word on wedding issues, you are their second-in-command; their right hand. You're Biden to their Obama, and you have the power to make decisions about how to handle minor skirmishes in their stead. Suppose the videographer is handing out business cards to everyone at the reception, or the band is taking a break just as the happy couple is about to cut the wedding cake? Reprimand the videographer; goose the band. The people who have been paid to perform services at the wedding are expected to behave professionally and respectfully and adhere to schedules. You have the authority to keep these professionals in line because a bride should never be pulled out of her first dance or romantic reverie to make sure they're handling their responsibilities. As the maid of honor, you have the job to handle on-site crises. Need a stronger arm? Ask the bride's mother. Nobody wants to mess with the bride's mother.

Knowing your duties as the MOH is necessary, but it's also important to understand the realistic parameters of your role. Even the best of friends and the meekest of people can turn into a

Bridezilla once that ring goes on her finger, and it's critical to put your foot down when she abuses or exploits you. You'll maintain your sanity and preserve your long-term friendship.

What Is Not a Part of Your Duties as MOH:

- **Writing thank-you notes.** We know of at least one bride who had the nerve to ask her MOH to begin composing her thank-you notes while she was on her honeymoon (you can't make this stuff up, folks). The maid of honor is not a secretary, assistant, or stenographer. Thank-you notes are a personal expression of gratitude from the recipient to the giver. If the bride doesn't understand that, we're not exactly sure why you're friends with her in the first place. The bride mentioned above? When her MOH politely declined, the bride stuck her mother with the task. For any bridesmaids who are studying psychology, keep in mind that participating in a wedding party is like lab work without having to turn in a notebook. You'll witness all kinds of dysfunctional family dynamics.

- **Concierge service.** We're not talking about getting the bride a cup of coffee while she gets her makeup done the morning of the wedding. We're talking about picking up dresses for her, gathering band information, hiring (or firing) a florist, and generally performing tasks that the bride should be doing herself. You're her aide and can assist her on the job. But you're not her errand boy (or girl).

- **Wedding planner**—unless you *are* a wedding planner and you have offered your services.

- **Couples therapist.** It's not your job to call the groom-to-be to tell him that his bride-to-be is pissed because his mother-in-law-to-be was offended by the bride's sister-in-law-to-be over whatever-the-hell-it-may-be . . . or something. You get the picture. Stay out of domestic disputes.

Your primary goal as the MOH is to relieve the bride of having to worry over too many details on her wedding day. This responsibility extends to preempting or solving problems that may arise— minor and major. Be prepared for the mundane, such as helping the bride maneuver her hoop skirt into the bathroom stall, as well as the scary, like intercepting the groom's angry ex when she crashes the reception. (Did we mention you're a bouncer, too?) Many things can go wrong at a wedding and often do. You must be on the alert so the bride can enjoy her day. This is no job for the faint of heart. The key to being a successful maid of honor is a lot of preparation, organization, and a very, *very* good sense of humor.

4

The Bridesmaid's Timetable and Toolkit

Weddings and the weeks, months, and year(s) leading up to them can be a socially complex and emotionally charged time in a bride's life. No wonder she's pulling her hair out! Beware the trickle-down effect: Freneticism and hypersensitivity can be contagious and may lead to a distortion of reality by the bride, such as, "Oh my God, the reception hall only serves Vienna Roast coffee! They don't have Kona blend! The wedding is RUINED!!! Bwww-waaaahhhh!!!!" (Insert tears.) Or maybe you find yourself sending angry text messages to other bridesmaids because the tea-length bridesmaid gown the bride just picked out makes you look like you have cankles.

Sometimes brides just need a reality check. Sometimes you will, too. Just keep in mind that one day it will all be a memory, and we can promise you that no wedding ever sucked because of a little thing like coffee flavor or a hemline. Maybe a bad DJ . . . but that's not your problem.

Don't make the mistake of troubling yourself with imagined

motives, and don't complain to your coworkers about the daily irksome details of the wedding process—that's what Facebook is for. No, we're kidding. Don't put it on Facebook. Or tweet "I HATE BRIDES! #weddingssuck." Griping about the bride to everyone around you could result in your boyfriend developing an allergy to the word *wedding* and your colleagues avoiding you like the plague. And while you may forget that you ridiculed the notion of an orchestra and a band, and a dozen interactive food stations with a sommelier and cheese tastings and a sushi chef, your boyfriend or mother or future mother-in-law will be quick to remind you once you start planning the wedding of your dreams. You are better off biting your tongue and sharing your frustrations with a therapist so your words don't come back to haunt you and travel back to the bride's ears.

The surest way to keep the bride sane is to offer her assurance that she can rely on your support. You can't accomplish this by saying your bra doesn't work with the one-shoulder bridesmaid dress an hour before the photographer is ready for photos. The key to being a successful (and sane) bridesmaid is planning, planning, planning. Don't assume your shoe-repair shop will dye your white silk pumps the exact same rose-petal pink as your dress on the first try, or that your dress won't come back two sizes too small from the tailor's. With a little advanced preparation, you can glide through the bride's engagement period with minimal stress, avoiding those common (and not-so-common) pitfalls that can turn a joyous event into an excruciating memory. It's not your wedding, but you have to pull your own weight, perhaps as well as another bridesmaid's (see "The Slacker Bridesmaid" in Chapter 5). As a good bridal attendant, you have accepted a major role in the most important event (or if she's a serial bride, one of the biggest) in someone else's life. And because you're a good friend, you take your job seriously. There are about a hundred things you'll need to do to prepare for the big day. This timetable will help you stay sane and on track:

One Year to Nine Months Before the Wedding Day:

☐ Purchase engagement gift (optional). *TIP: While a gift is optional, a card is very thoughtful and may be something you'll want to send to the bride regardless.*

☐ Attend engagement party. (This is often thrown by the parents, close friends who aren't necessarily in the wedding party, or the couple themselves.)

☐ If everyone in the wedding party is on Facebook, consider setting up a private page for the attendants. Let the wedding excitement commence!

Six Months Before:

☐ Provide your dress measurements to the bride, MOH, or designated bridal salon for dress ordering. If you're an OOTA (out-of-town attendant), this time frame will allow for delivery of the dress to your home, leaving plenty of time for alterations and corrections to any major mix-ups, like your getting Cousin Marjorie's size 16 gown and her getting your size 8. Great sites like weddingtonway.com and bellabridesmaid.com have made shopping online for bridesmaid dresses simple, especially as a group. But be prepared for wait times, and leave lots of extra time for necessary returns.

☐ If you're really lucky and the bride lets you choose your own dress for the wedding, start searching for your gown. Believe it or not, finding just the right dress is impossible—especially when you *have* to find one (it's the Murphy's Law of shopping). To make it doubly difficult, stores don't carry summer dresses in summertime. They carry them in early spring. Don't wait until the last minute to find a dress, or the selection will be paltry.

☐ Start planning the bridal shower. (See Chapter 7, "The Bridal Shower.")

Three Months Before:

☐ Pick up and pay for your bridesmaid gown.

☐ Take the gown to the tailor for any alterations. Resolve to stay the same weight until the day after the wedding.

☐ Purchase your shoes, as per the bride's color and style requests. If you have to dye them, three months allows for plenty of time so they can be done to match your dress, if necessary. Consider going a half size *up* so you can insert some comfy and squishy foot cushions. These aren't your grandma's foot cushions, either! These babies are made of gel, they're invisible, and they seriously help take the burn off your feet when you're dancing till dawn.

☐ Schedule a hair salon appointment for the wedding day if you're having your hair blown out or professionally styled (optional).

☐ Make arrangements for flights and accommodations if you're an OOTA. Hotels fill up quickly, and chances are that even if the bride and groom have reserved a block of rooms at the group rate, there is a deadline for reservations.

☐ Make plans for the bachelorette party to be held no less than one week prior to the wedding. (See Chapter 8, "The Bachelorette Party/Weekend.") You'll feel queasy enough on the day of the wedding when nosy guests interrogate you about your own love life without the added effects of a bad hangover.

☐ Maid of honor discusses with bridesmaids whether they'd like to present the bride with a gift from them at the bridesmaid luncheon or the rehearsal dinner. (See Chapter 3, "The Maid of Honor," optional.)

☐ Maid of honor helps the bride order wedding welcome bags for guests and plans what to stash inside them: For a destination wedding, consider local treats, a map, and a weekend itinerary. These can be custom ordered at weddingchicks.com (so can save-the-date wedding hankies).

One Month Before:

- ☐ Book a manicure/pedicure appointment (if you don't plan on doing your own nails). Fresh, clean-looking hands and fingernails are a bridesmaid must on wedding day!

- ☐ Try on your dress and make sure you have the right undergarments. A creeping underwear line could ruin your look. If you go for a full-body Spanx or other type of results wear, make sure it has snaps or loops at the crotch. No, not so you can get wild in the coatroom with that groom's college roommate. It's so you can pee without slipping off your whole outfit. Trust us. It's a necessity. And if you get lucky, well . . .

- ☐ Plan your outfit for the rehearsal dinner. Find out whether it will be a casual or dressy affair and dress accordingly.

- ☐ Pick up your shoes at the shoe shop where you've had them dyed and re-dyed four times before getting that rose-petal-pink shade right.

- ☐ Purchase a wedding gift. Technically, you have up to one year after the wedding to give a gift. Decide if you want to take a gift to the wedding or have it sent at a later date. If you've already laid out a good deal of cash for this event, you may want to save a little each month and purchase the gift later on. Even better? Go in on a gift with a fellow guest or bridesmaid.

☐ Get your hair cut. Do *not* get your hair cut on the day of the wedding or even the day before. A bad haircut can dampen your spirits. Schedule your haircut no less than a month before the wedding and *don't* try anything too drastic. This is not the time to experiment with that pixie cut that looks so good on, well, somebody else.

Two Weeks Before:

☐ Scuff your shoes. Take them outside for a stroll—in nice weather, of course—and walk around on the sidewalk or an asphalt road. Do a little soft-shoe number for your neighbors if you'd like, but just scratch up the soles so that when you wear them at the reception, you don't slide off the dance floor and into the punch bowl. Or get a good shoemaker to match a rubber sole to the shoe's sole color to ensure that you won't slip.

☐ Buy shoe inserts. Another option is Dr. Scholl's blister tape. You put this on the inside of your shoes wherever they rub, and it helps prevent blisters. This stuff is miraculous.

☐ Attend the bridal luncheon (if the bride is throwing one).

☐ If you're going to have a facial, do it now! We know plenty of overzealous brides and bridesmaids who, in pursuit of perfection for the wedding, have gotten facials a day or two before the big event. Big mistake. BIG! HUGE! Sure, your skin will glow, but it will also be covered in nasty blotches and red marks where the facialist picked and picked and picked. Allow time for your face to fully heal and that healthy, clean glow to shine all over.

One Week Before:

☐ Assemble the contents of your Bridesmaid's Toolkit.

☐ Confirm transportation and directions to the ceremony, from the ceremony to the reception site (if it's different), and from the reception to home. You'll probably be drinking and you should NOT be driving!

☐ Make sure you have all additional items you'll need for the wedding (hosiery, hair accessories, gloves, and so on. See Wedding Day Checklist, Chapter 10, pages 170–71).

The Day Before:

☐ Get a manicure and pedicure, or do them yourself. This is one beauty treatment that SHOULD be done either the day before or ON the day of the wedding. Chips and dry cuticles are a beauty don't. You may want to get a gel manicure prior to the bachelorette party, since that kind of nail treatment has the staying power to last through the wedding.

☐ Steam or press your dress if necessary, and hang it up where it won't get wrinkled.

☐ Go to bed early. Yes, get off Facebook, turn off your phone, shut down on Twitter, and go to sleep!

The Day of the Event:

☐ See Chapter 10, "At the Wedding!"

☐ Eat a good breakfast.

☐ Meditate or toss salt over your shoulder.

The Bridesmaid's Toolkit

Now that you know about all the typical responsibilities of a bridesmaid, you should be prepared for the atypical tasks—those little unplanned issues that invariably crop up.

The purpose of being an attendant is to attend to the bride—natch. She is your cause, your purpose, your raison d'etre. And even if she isn't, she thinks she is, and you love her, so just go with it. The finest bridesmaids are equipped for any complication, nuisance, or snafu that can (and usually will) arise at or right before the wedding. You are the bride's emergency hotline, and you need to be ready for any emergency, medical or otherwise. We're not talking CPR, although if cold feet are a problem, it wouldn't hurt to know a little. We're talking about having a little toolkit packed with all the things you might need to help the bride in a critical moment to head disaster off at the pass. A week to at least forty-eight hours before the wedding, gather the following items and throw them into a bag, box, or toolkit of sorts. This will be your arsenal and will ensure you're ready for almost any wedding incident—good, bad, or just plain ugly:

- **Aspirin and/or ibuprofen.** Boring toasts, mixing your liquor (savvy bridesmaids know wine + vodka = headache), loud music, *throb, throb, throb.* You don't want to let a headache stand in the way of a good time.

- **Adhesive bandages.** Uncomfortable shoes, bad dancers, standing up all night. Bring several different sizes and shapes for cuts and blisters. The best are the cushiony blister ones.

- **Gel shoe inserts.** These miracle gel pads are the best invention since boob tape! Thank you, Dr. Scholl's (although there are cheaper knock-off versions). With these spongy puppies in your shoes fighting foot fatigue and the "burning ball" (of your feet), you might actually dance the night away! They even make inserts for open-toe shoes and you can't see them at all. Simply genius. Note: Make sure your shoes are a half size larger or at least have room in them for your foot and the inserts or you'll risk making your shoes too tight.

- **Nasal spray.** Especially for outdoor weddings held at the height of hay fever season. A runny nose is not attractive on any member of the wedding party. Which brings us to—

- **Tissues.** If you do get that runny nose, using the back of your hand just won't do, especially when you're expected to shake hands in the receiving line. And you can use a tissue to blot your lipstick so it doesn't rub off on your teeth.

- **White medical tape.** It's shiny, made of cloth, and almost looks like some kind of wedding trim. It's perfect for everything from taping bridal boo-boos to holding down headpiece fabric.

- **Needle, thread, and scissors.** Buttons pop off, hems rip, and tags may need to be removed. If you have the time, these items can be lifesavers.

- **Safety pins.** Because chances are you *won't* have the time to make real repairs. Bring a variety of sizes from the cute teeny-tiny ones to the major punk-rocker bad boys. With the right-size safety pin, you can hold just about anything together, from flimsy spaghetti straps and ripped lace to stretched seams and fallen hems. Bridal gowns and bridesmaid dresses get stomped on, smushed, yanked, and caught on flimsy trellises with cascading greenery. Likewise, one good turn on the dance floor and the slit of your dress reveals your derrière to the world. Safety pins are essential in any Bridesmaid's Toolkit.

- **Nail file.** Ragged nails can snag tulle and silk. Snags are bad.

- **Clear nail polish.** Nails chip and stockings run. These are facts of life. Clear nail polish is the sure fix for both.

- **Smelling salts.** When emotions run high, such as at a wedding, people can keel over.

- **Double-stick boob tape.** Perfect for holding dresses in place and avoiding unintentional side boob. Or whole boob.

- **Oil-blotting cloths.** As a bridesmaid, you should shine, but your face shouldn't. These little beauty secrets are perfect for blotting excess oil off your (and the bride's) nose, forehead, and chin.

- **Deodorant.** Because you don't want to be smelly. It's not ladylike.

- **Deodorant eraser.** Because in your quest to avoid being smelly, you might get deodorant, a stubborn stain, on your navy blue satin dress. This will help.

- **Instant stain remover.** God forbid the bride needs this, but you'll want to have it at your fingertips in case lipstick or toothpaste lands where it shouldn't.

- **Breath strips or mints.** Again, smelly isn't sexy. And you might want to engage in an intimate conversation with a cute cousin of the groom without unintentionally announcing you ate a lot of spanakopita

- **Disposable toothbrush.** Tiny, compact, and disposable, these brilliant little inventions have toothpaste already in the brush and, hence, are also perfect for garlic-loving attendants.

- **Bobby pins (aka hairpins).** Bring at least ten of these, and you may want to find a nice jeweled pin or barrette besides the basic brown or black, because no matter how many pins Jacques-Paul crisscrossed into your elaborate updo, rest assured that the first time your partner dips you on the dance floor, your hair will spring free.

- **Tampons and panty liners.** It doesn't matter if the last day of your period was yesterday. Especially if you'll be wearing white or light colors. Better to be ready than to be sorry.

- **Compact mirror.** All that smooching and being smooched is enough to make any flower wilt. Perfect for quick touch-ups for the bride and you.

- **Condoms.** Because you never know. And in Girl Scouts, or in college, you learned to always be prepared.

Keep your toolkit under the front pew at the ceremony, in the bride's room at the reception hall, or under your table. Wherever you are, the kit should be within arm's reach. This kit is your best friend (next to the bride, of course).

5

Functioning as a Team: What Kind of Bridesmaid Are You?

A happy bridesmaid makes a happy bride.
—ALFRED LORD TENNYSON

The most important thing you can do as a bridesmaid is support the bride and keep drama and conflict at bay. At the engagement party, when you hear her future mother-in-law whisper too loudly to a relative that her son could have married a doctor, lead the bride away from the harpies while commenting that you've observed how lovingly the groom has been gazing at her that evening. If the bride takes her dieting to extremes in the weeks before the wedding, remind her that men like curves, and introduce her to some delicious smoothie recipes. And if there's a bridesmaid who is a tad too bossy or one whose taste you find outright offensive, you most definitely do not share this with the bride; find a way to push aside any differences and work together.

Keep in mind that our friends often reflect different facets of our personalities. You may have been college roommates with the bride and enjoyed some wild spring-break vacations together—you still have the empty tequila bottle with incriminating Polaroids stuffed inside that the two of you dubbed the Agave Time Capsule.

Perhaps another bridesmaid bonded with her as a first-year associate at a corporate law firm and jokes with her in Latin. Then there's her cousin from the Jersey Shore who taught her how to expertly apply fake eyelashes. When you meet these other women, you may find yourself wondering how all of you will ever come together as a team. But to support your mutual friend, you *will* find a way. Getting along with the other bridesmaids is one of the most fundamental ways you can turn the bride's hopes and dreams into a magical reality.

Ask yourself if your dearest friends would immediately bond with one another if put in a situation with a common task. Probably not, but you cherish each one for her uniqueness and spirit, and you know that every individual has a different strength to contribute. Consider that as much as the bride loves you, it wouldn't be helpful for her to have *five* of you in her wedding party. Figure out the innate talents of each bridesmaid and how those assets might be used to assist the bride as she prepares for the big day. Think of it like a season of *Celebrity Apprentice*, but you won't have to cooperate with a less-famous Baldwin brother or an addled former basketball player.

Go Team!

The Bridal Party is the only group of people in life that brings together such disparate personalities, usually with only one thing in common—the bride—to work as a team for one common cause. There are bound to be conflicts and personality clashes, and it will be clear, possibly by the end of the engagement party, that you aren't all going to be friends. But you have to work together to rise above the chaos of the wedding planning and form a united front. You must not give in to any petty behavior, no matter how many of your buttons are being pushed. And while this sounds like you should avoid conflict and drama at all costs, you must not be a passive bystander either.

So, in addition to traditional duties and playing the role of a diplomat, a bridesmaid also needs be mindful of flagging spirits on the team. Unreturned phone calls, single-letter responses to texts, ignored e-mails, and not a single Favorite of your tweet *"WOOT! WOOT! Psyched for Erin's bachelorette party tonight!"* are signs that quiet outrage may have infected the group. Take stock of how much time and money the bridesmaids have been asked to contribute already. The tedium of fittings at the bridal salon, the drudgery of finding a stick-on bra for double Ds, and the numbing practice of sympathetically listening to the bride's latest litany of complaints can get to even the most laid-back of bridesmaids.

Sometimes a force much darker than typical wedding weariness is at work and making all the bridesmaids feel uncomfortable. Sometimes there's that problem bridesmaid who has always been competitive with the bride or for the bride's attention. If this is your situation, we're really sorry because it sucks. It's often better to gather and discuss rather than suppress and splinter. Identify shared values and goals: the bride's happiness and a successful wedding. In the case of a friend or relative who is not a part of the bridal party but is inserting herself and creating drama, you have to learn to tune out negativity and ignore such a toxic person. Giving in to any trash talk or tantrums will only encourage such behavior. As trying as it may be in the beginning to cheerfully carry on with your wedding obligations and preparations as though there isn't a thorn in your and the bride's side, it'll become your default setting before you know it.

While revelry and practical jokes at the bridal shower can relieve tension and promote camaraderie, you may need a mood elevator sooner. A little levity could be a quick fix. Morale boosting and wedding-party bonding can take the form of a girls' night out, a trip to the nail salon, or even a group bull session in which each bridesmaid can vent her frustrations with the prenuptial process (please set appropriate boundaries so no one goes off the rails). Try to organize a dinner or a lunch, or meet for cocktails.

Even a night at a bridesmaid's home watching such movies as *Bridesmaids* or *27 Dresses* can help let off group steam. The lesser-known *Catered Affair* (1956) is fun for some campy laughs— an ambitious Bette Davis plans an extravagant wedding for daughter Debbie Reynolds that her husband, Ernest Borgnine, can't afford. (Take note how the mother-of-the-bride stereotype has pretty much remained the same over the past fifty years, and tease accordingly. A lively MOB- or MIL-bashing is always good for bridesmaid bonding.) If some of the attendants live in other cities, it may not be possible to meet the other bridesmaids (or bridesmen—more on that later) before the bachelorette party. Try to arrange a group video-conference using Skype to introduce yourselves.

Whether the bride has just you and her maid of honor or you and eight sorority sisters (her friend since kindergarten who now feels like the odd man out with these women who speak in sorority code), you want to find a way to work together and function as a team. Trust us, if you can manage this, you will have a much more rewarding experience, and the bride will be grateful. Don't think for a minute that she doesn't realize how difficult the women in her life can be.

The key to getting along is to acknowledge that everyone is different and coming from a different perspective. Recognize that there will be some challenges, and remember the common goal that should unite you: supporting the bride. It may help your team-working efforts to figure out which category of bridesmaid you and perhaps your other counterparts fit into.

TYPE-A BRIDESMAID

As soon as you got the call, you created a spreadsheet in Excel. Your iPhone case matches your iPad cover. You know which colors and styles will be most flattering for you and your fellow brides-maids, and you're going to persuade the bride to take your advice for the good of all. And yes, it just so happens you have a dress in that color and style from the last wedding in which you served as a bridesmaid. You have strong opinions about what is the best venue for a bridal shower or bachelorette party, and you have to remind yourself to feign interest in the opinions of the other bridesmaids. If everyone would just do it your way, it would save a lot of time and energy, and things would go much more smoothly! On your laptop, you've already bookmarked the webpage with the couple's wedding registry. If you recognize yourself as the Type-A Bridesmaid, take deep breaths and force yourself to listen to the other bridesmaids' ideas. Someone may actually have one you haven't thought of already!

How to get the Type-A Bridesmaid to chill: Surprise her with an unexpected small gift to remind her that many of life's delights are serendipitous.

THE FIRST-TIME BRIDESMAID

You're either dreading the experience, mildly curious, or full of enthusiasm but not sure where to start. You're feeling anxious about what the tally will be for travel/clothing/presents but don't want to appear gauche by asking how the other bridesmaids can afford all those expenses. You're hoping it will all work out somehow. You can't decide whether it would be fun to catch the bridal bouquet or humiliating. You're wondering if your boyfriend will feel pressured about your own relationship if you invite him as your plus one. If you are a First-Time Bridesmaid, you'll want to pay particular attention to the chapters detailing budgets and the essential toolkit.

How to reassure a First-Time Bridesmaid: Share stories of your first walk down the aisle as one of eight bridesmaids wearing orange and black for a wedding on Halloween and how hilarious it is to look at those photos now.

THE SERIAL BRIDESMAID

You've been an attendant at least three times, and you figure you could do it in your sleep. You can predict which relative will make the embarrassing toast, and you can estimate the trajectory of the bouquet by its shape and size: Lilies soar and peonies plop. Most of your vacation days have been used for long weekends, preparing or recovering from wedding-related travels. Lately you've been stewing over things that are less crystal clear, like when it will be your turn to be the bride. You've been paying it forward and paying your dues with nine taffeta dresses hanging in your closet. When is the universe going to reward you? You've debated whether you should put forth a little less effort for others. Don't sleepwalk your way through this one! Reach out to your fellow bridesmaids, and use your expertise to help plan an unforgettable bachelorette party or bridal shower. If you are a repeat bridesmaid, it's easy to either lose enthusiasm for some of the planning or to exert your expertise. Be mindful of these extremes and make an effort to stay involved without imposing your ideas on others.

How to focus a Serial Bridesmaid: Ask her what was the most enjoyable bridal shower or bachelorette party that she's attended and discuss whether to incorporate elements into the shower and party you are planning for this bride.

THE ROMANTIC

You get caught up in the details but don't notice the competing egos among the other bridesmaids. You enjoy the process of helping the bride create a beautiful day of celebration. Isn't this what life is all about—making dreams a reality? And what could be more fulfilling than helping a friend make her dream come true? You understand that a special event full of love and laughter can create warm memories for a lifetime, and you're thrilled to be a part of it. You're hoping the bride will arrange to have white doves or butterflies released after the ceremony. Your favorite movies all have weddings in them. People may joke that brides are seeking fairy-tale weddings, but you recognize that fairy tales have an enduring power. If you recognize yourself as a romantic among cynics, try not to get bummed out by their negativity or let your feelings be bruised by jabs about unicorns and rainbows. You can remind them of some of the inspiring, enduring love matches throughout the centuries, and maybe you'll open their eyes to why it's worth celebrating when two souls come together.

How to bring the Romantic down to earth: Ask her to take charge of creating a scrapbook of the wedding journey that the bridesmaids can present to the bride at the wedding.

THE CYNIC/THE RELUCTANT BRIDESMAID

You're not too crazy about the groom, you remember the bride's previous engagement, you wonder if there's a prenup, and you don't understand why couples fritter away money on a wedding when they could put the money toward a down payment. You're thinking, *Why did she ask me anyway? I certainly have better things to do with my money and time!* Well, Ms. Mope, stop standing on the sidelines and join the party! For once in your life, get on the bandwagon and see what the action looks like. A change in perspective could do you good.

If you recognize yourself as a cynical bridesmaid, why not take the bride to lunch and listen to the story of how she met the groom and when she realized she loved him? Since you are the bride's friend, you probably have a hazy memory of these things happening, but due to disinterest (and your cynicism), didn't give them much credence. The bride will be touched by your interest, and it is a generous thing to do, to listen to another woman's retelling of her love story. You may decide it is enough that your friend has found some happiness in sharing her life with another soul and that you don't need to appoint yourself the judge of whether the groom is worthy of her. Without that burden, you'll feel lighter and may start to enjoy yourself more—in general, not just during the wedding planning and celebrations.

How to soften the Cynic: Put her in charge of finding a keepsake (sentimental) gift from the bridesmaids, perhaps a vintage locket, to present to the bride.

THE PARTY GIRL

You're focused on having a good time. Your first thought after the call was, *Are the groomsmen single and hot?* You'll perform your duties with gusto, with an emphasis on the bachelorette party. You're always groomed and ready for a photo op. Let the cameras flash! You'll make certain the bride has a blast during her last months as a single lady. You're doing your best not to dwell on self- ish thoughts that this marks an ending, not a beginning, for your former fun partner in crime. At the reception, you'll know the bartender by name, and you'll be the first one on the dance floor after the newlyweds. You know a hundred ways to break the ice (and know it can sometimes be more fun to melt it), and you do it all with your own inimitable joie de vivre.

If you are the Party Girl, take a moment to consider when to tone down your behavior. Think twice before throwing a come- hither glance at a handsome guest who might be married. You don't want to put the bride in the position of having to apologize to another guest for something you've done. Think of yourself as a rare vintage that is too valuable to be passed around and swilled. Hold yourself in reserve for someone who sees you for more than a pretty face and a good time.

How to handle the Party Girl: Let her channel her crazy into planning the bachelorette party and ask her to research yelp.com for the most highly rated local bondsmen, and learn how to post a bond. Remind her nobody looks her best in a mug shot.

THE DIVA

Sometimes there's a bridesmaid who is Type-A, the Cynic, and the Party Girl all rolled into one moody package with her own stormy weather system. That's the Diva. You've been called a maneater, a femme fatale, a cougar, and a witch with a capital *B*, and you wear all those labels with pride. You figure it's better to be talked about than overlooked, and everyone is just jealous. You wish the bride had been a little more discerning when choosing her future husband and her other friends, but most people don't adhere to the high standards you do. You feel a pang of alarm that the bride will be the one in the spotlight, but you feel better when you realize that no one in the wedding party is as photogenic as you. You love the bride dearly, but that doesn't mean you're going to start hugging all her relatives or accepting Friend requests on Facebook from the other bridesmaids. If you are the Diva, use your sense of style and experience with caterers to plan the bridal shower. You, more than anyone, can make it an elegant affair to remember. Keep in mind it's unlikely that a dashing captain of industry is going to walk into the room and in your view just beyond the shoulder of the guest you're conversing with. And if one does, you wouldn't want to be the first to greet him, would you? Focus your attention on the person sharing thoughts with you and take the time to learn what his or her gifts are. The person in front of you may prove to be more valuable to you than you'd originally estimated.

How to rein in the Diva: Tell her the bride chose her for her leadership qualities but is worried some of the other attendants might be intimidated by her.

How to get the Diva to focus on the wedding festivities rather than herself: Casually remark you heard that *Town & Country* will be covering the wedding with a photographer at the ceremony, and they've asked for details about the bridal shower.

THE RELATIVE

You are the bride's cousin or future sister-in-law, and you suspect there was some strong-arming that led to your appointment, or a sense of obligation. Or your younger or older sister wanted you to stand at her side on the most pivotal day of her life. However close you are to the bride, or if you're welcoming her as a new member of the family, you may feel ill at ease among her longtime friends.

If you are a non-blood relative who feels a little on the periphery of festivities, don't make yourself more of an outsider by talking about this. Allow yourself to bond with the other women and let the bride know how grateful you are to stand by her side. One thoughtful gesture could involve asking the bride's mother or sister if there is treat she loved as a child and arrange for it to be served at the bridal shower (butterscotch pudding) or the bachelorette party (Devil Dogs). If you're a blood relative who has shared a long history with the bride, why not acknowledge this with a sentimental gift. Maybe there's a favorite cookbook your grandmother has that is now out of print and you could find it at abebooks.com, alibris.com, or ebay.com. Have Nana add her notes about how she's made those dishes even better with additional spices or about the family occasions at which she has served them (for example, the bride's christening).

How to make the Relative feel included: Ask her to share a family tradition or her knowledge about a unique skill or interest the bride has that might be incorporated into one of the shower themes or games. For example, Allison's cousin mentioned that Allison used to love kayaking at summer camp and the cousin recently found out that the groom also enjoyed camping as a child. Her attendants were inspired to throw the shower as a picnic at a local campground and bought a kayak as a group present. They filled it with camping gear (compass, fleece jacket, whistle, waterproof lighter, mini binoculars, bandanna, paddling gloves) and had a contest that involved remembering the lyrics to campfire songs.

THE SLACKER BRIDESMAID

Is the bachelorette party really this weekend? Months ago, you saw a bunch of e-mails zipping back and forth with suggestions about party-theme ideas from names you didn't recognize, and your eyes glazed over at the exhaustive details each time you ventured to open one. Well, you might have to miss the party. You don't get so revved up about drinking and watching men strip—that's what they do at bachelorette parties, right?—but you'll definitely be at the wedding! You're going to call the bride and just ask her to read the invitation to you because you can't find it, and you've already searched all the usual corners you stash the this-can-wait stuff. It was so long ago . . . maybe later you'll check the pockets of the coat you were wearing about the time it arrived.

If you're the Slacker, stick a corkboard on the back of your front door so you see it each time you leave your home. Put all your reminders on neatly spaced Post-its.

How to motivate the Slacker bridesmaid: You can't, and you might be better off not relying on her to help plan the shower or bachelorette party. What you can do for the sake of the bride is keep reminding the Slacker when the actual wedding is taking place, and where, so she remembers to show up. Under no circumstances should the Slacker bridesmaid be put in charge of recording the shower gifts.

THE WALLFLOWER

You want to participate, and you have ideas you'd like to share, but everyone seems to speak at a higher decibel and jumps right in. Whatever happened to taking turns and listening to others? That's how it works in the book club you and the bride belong to. You realize the bride appreciates your ability to listen and your steadfast loyalty. You'd rather fold origami swans for three hours than have to make a toast or dance with Uncle Jerry. If you are the Wallflower: Volunteer to help address the invitations or keep track of vendor contracts for the bride.

How to encourage the Wallflower: Seek out her opinions and listen to her thoughts. Don't assume because she is silent that she has nothing to say.

THE BRIDESMAN

In modern weddings, sometimes the bride wants a guy friend to participate in the bridal party. You may be her childhood next-door neighbor who's like a brother to her, or her Thursday night bingo partner. Whether you are straight or gay, your presence is most likely going to make the other women feel a little more sparkly if you're gallant and attentive. In rare cases there may be a sourpuss who perceives you as an invader of a female domain, but politeness and a gentle sense of humor should neutralize her. If you are the Bridesman: Be chivalrous, and don't fool around with any of the bridesmaids. If you want to flirt, then keep it light and flirt with all of them, not just the lovely ones.

How to keep the Bridesman from feeling like the odd man out: Include him in all the planning and take time to explain some of the more esoteric rituals of female bonding, like the bow bonnet at the shower.

When you get together with the other bridesmaids, whether in person or via phone or e-mail, ask one another what you love most about the bride, and share some anecdotes that highlight her attributes and the good times you've had, how she's stuck with you through thick and thin. Brainstorm and troubleshoot together. Did she choose an outdoor wedding during hurricane season because she was able to get her first-choice venue at a better rate? Be prepared with matching umbrellas and create a phone chain to alert guests in case the ceremony has to be moved to another location at the last minute. Share this nugget of wisdom from one of the stars of the movie *Bridesmaids*, the comedienne and actress Melissa McCarthy. Her theory on how best to support the bride: "Know her favorite cocktail—and when she needs it."

No matter what kind of bridesmaid you are, reflect on this timeless advice from *The Social Mirror: A Complete Treatise on the Laws, Rules and Usages that Govern Our Most Refined Homes and Social Circles*, a classic book on etiquette:

> *The good manners of any person are an inspiration*
> *to all those with whom he comes in contact. They are*
> *to the eye what the eloquence of speech is to the ear.*
> *Subdued by their charm, he who is ordinarily careless*
> *and rude becomes, for the time being, courteous and*
> *refined; for manners are learned by example.*

Etiquette is thinking before you speak or act, and making sure kind impulses guide you. Let courtesy, taste, and kindness be your guides. The rules of etiquette may sometimes seem inflexible but should be viewed as a helpful road map across unfamiliar territory, or simply the double yellow line on a road well traveled. Protocol tells you through which door to make an entrance; etiquette advises you how and to whom you introduce yourself, or wait for an introduction to, once you are inside.

Traditions change, but following are some vignettes with basic rules for bridesmaids to remember, along with practices you may want to follow or departures from the script that you may want to avoid.

The bridesmaid is not expected to respond to the wedding invitation she receives. After she has confirmed that she will be a bridesmaid, it is understood that she will attend the wedding. However, if the invitation response lists meal options, then complete and return the response card.

- A Romantic Bridesmaid uses the invitation to begin a scrapbook for the couple that she'll collaborate on with the other bridesmaids and present to the bride at the shower.

- The Cynical Bridesmaid tosses the invitation into a drawer with her takeout menus and the ten other wedding invitations that have arrived in the mail this year.

Bridesmaids assure the bride that the bridesmaid's dress she has selected is stunning and much nicer than any they've had to wear previously.

- The Diva Bridesmaid starts a campaign to revolt and e-mails photos of a more glamorous dress to her fellow bridesmaids.

- The Bridesman lucks out and gets to wear a tie that matches the color of the bridesmaid dresses.

- The Party Girl surreptitiously has the seamstress raise the hem by five inches.

Bridesmaids cooperate with one another.

- The Type-A Bridesmaid has already introduced the other bridesmaids to doodle.com to plan dates for the shower and bachelorette party.

- The Slacker Bridesmaid has no idea who the other bridesmaids are and never responds to a single email.

Bridesmaids assist the bride with wedding-related errands and tasks, such as addressing the envelopes if a calligrapher is not in the bride's budget

- The Relative Bridesmaid has the addresses of everyone who needs to be sent an invitation.

- The Party Girl Bridesmaid leaves traces of her lipstick on each envelope she seals.

Having a grasp of your role in the bridal party as well as understanding wedding etiquette is essential to your success as a bridesmaid. Your performance is a way to express your respect and love for the bride. Use these guidelines to express your awareness of the bride's concerns and needs at this tumultuous time. When in doubt, decide upon the most commonsensical and kind solution and take action, and above all, maintain a sense of humor.

6

The Gear and the Look

The principal duty of the brides-maid is to look
pretty, and not out-shine the bride. She may wear
a dainty costume of white or some delicate tint, not
of so rich a fabric as the bride's, and without a
train. Dressy hats or bonnets are often worn . . .

—ROSE CLEVELAND, *The Social Mirror*

For any of life's milestones celebrated with a ceremony, there is the costume de rigueur, attire that is acceptable and expected. At this stage in your life, you have a pretty good sense of what to wear on any given occasion. You wouldn't wear a tracksuit to a baptism or a red sundress to a funeral. Most likely you own a lovely cocktail dress that would be perfect for the upcoming wedding. But you can't wear that, because you're in the wedding party, and the bride gets to choose your dress. And on the off chance the bride allows you to choose, well, she'll have to approve. That's just the way it is. It's her wedding. Think of the bride as the director, screen-writer, and leading actress of a movie in which she has given you a supporting role. Your bridesmaid's dress is a costume in a production, not an expression of who you are. Do you think Jodie Foster let Mel Gibson dress himself in her film *The Beaver*? Well, maybe she did, but you get our point.

This is the time when you must set aside your own aesthetic

preferences. To make this process as smooth as can be, first find out as early as possible what dress the bride has chosen for her attendants. It's difficult to find forest green dresses with long sleeves in June, and that may be what the bride has her heart set on for her October wedding. Ideally, she'll choose the dress or style and color, and let her bridesmaids and maid of honor know while it's still possible to purchase the dress (if she's chosen one from a large retailer like J. Crew). If the bride has chosen a dress from a wedding salon, availability is less of an issue because the salon will be ready to order the number of dresses she tells them she needs; they'll just be waiting for the bridesmaids' measurements, or if they live locally, for them to come in for a fitting.

While in most traditional ceremonies, all the bridesmaids will wear matching dresses, there is a new trend in modern weddings of brides choosing one color and fabric from a designer that offers different styles. If the bride is considering this option, you might suggest one of these retailers to her:

weddingtonway.com
jcrew.com
dessy.com
twobirdsbridesmaids.com
annaelyse.com
jordanfashions.com
donna-morgan.com
erinfetherston.com

Most bridesmaids welcome the opportunity to select a flattering style. One of our favorite sites, weddingtonway.com, even has a feature that enables the bride to invite her bridesmaids to look at her first-, second-, and third-choice dresses and comment/vote on them, as well as a body-type option that suggests the most becoming styles for a particular shape.

If given the opportunity to choose your own style, take an honest look at your body and examine all your options and determine the cut that will most flatter your shape. Ask yourself the following questions and tips when determining the right cut:

WHAT IS MY BODY TYPE?

You've heard of women being shaped like pears or apples, right? A pear shape is smaller on top and larger on the bottom. An apple is thicker in the midsection. Understanding if your body type falls into either of these categories is key to dressing fabulously. Okay, maybe you're a swimsuit model, and you look good in everything. Well, good for you. You can sit your skinny °ss down and eat a brownie. We'll get to you later.

FULL-FIGURED

- Do you have loads of va-va in your voom? If you're full-figured and want to flaunt it, look for a dress that's fitted in the waist, ruched in the thigh area, and shows off your curves from head to toe.

- A fitted shift can also be a great option with the right foundation garment.

- Want to hide your curves? (Don't feel ashamed of your assets! Consider the many examples of voluptuous gals considered gorgeous: Adele, Beyoncé, Kate Upton, Jennifer Lopez, Kate Winslet, Christina Hendricks, Marilyn Monroe.) If you're not confident about your womanly shape, consider a dress with an A-line skirt. It's a beautiful and flirty alternative to fitted. And remember, knowing you're beautiful is the key to looking radiant!

Do I have big boobs?

If so, one of the most important things you can do is find a dress that is bra-friendly. You need to get support and be able to dance without a Janet Jackson wardrobe malfunction. Here are some tips:

- Don't cover up from the neck down. For example, don't wear a chunky necklace over a high neckline. It will double the appearance of your chest.

- Consider a dress with a V in front and in back. This double V creates a sexy look while offering coverage.

- Halters are a great option—you can get support and lift from the halter.

- Backless dresses = BAD

- Strapless dresses are iffy. Ask yourself how comfortable you feel in your strapless bra. Foundation is the key to looking great in your dress, so if you think your girls need to be strapped in, avoid this look and go for another option. If the bride has chosen strapless dresses for her attendants, explain to her why this style of dress may not be ideal for your body type and suggest a matching dress that offers more support, which will look better in the wedding photos.

AM I PETITE?

- Avoid an empire-waist dress. You won't have a shape, and you'll be drowning in fabric.

- Strapless is great. If you have control of the dress length, keep it above the knee. Below the knee can also make you look overwhelmed.

- Try to keep the dress top more fitted to your body.

AM I PEAR-SHAPED?

- An empire-waist dress can be lovely on you. As with a petite figure, try to find a dress that is more fitted to your body on top so you can flaunt that beautiful décolletage!

AM I PREGNANT?

Maybe you just found out you're pregnant, and maybe you'll be ready to pop at the wedding. Either way, don't let that sway you from being in the wedding party. Pregnant bridesmaids are beautiful. And lucky for the bride! Personally, we don't understand brides who don't want pregnant bridesmaids in the wedding party. What's lovely about a wedding is the opportunity for the bride to bring all the people she loves together in one place for one day or one weekend. It's literally a completely unique event—never again will this group of people come together in the same place for her. It would be a shame not to include those she loves and who matter most just because they aren't at their most photogenic in life. Show off that bump in an empire-waist version of the bridesmaid dress!

If the bride is ordering from a local salon, ideally she'll take a few attendants with her so you can see which styles suit which body shapes. And when ordering from a high-end designer, it's best to do it all at once to ensure there is no variation in dye lot. The salon visit will take from one to two hours, and the boutique's seamstress will take hip, waist, and bust measurements. If you aren't near the salon but must provide measurements, make sure you get a tailor or someone familiar with taking measurements to do you the favor. Do not attempt to figure out your own measurements. Also be aware that for custom-made gowns, the measurements will vary from what might be your size in ready-to-wear. Regular delivery time for most designers is twelve weeks.

We love this advice and think you should keep it tucked in the back of your mind or purse when you're going through the process of buying a bridesmaid dress for a close friend's wedding: "A wedding should be about love and the joy of sharing with people who are important. Let the dress shopping be an opportunity to come together and have fun with the bride!" —Ilana Stern, founder, weddingtonway.com

Some brides will even create a Pinterest board and post a few different options from various designers within the same color palette, offering bridesmaids more freedom in picking out a dress that is most suited for them. And we've even heard of brides opting for a wild-card approach, trusting their bridesmaids to show up at the ceremony wearing something fabulous. You may already know what colors the bride has chosen, but definitely attempt to see the fabric in person, as computer screens don't always provide the true color.

Look on the bright side: you have an excuse to buy a new dress. Or if you're lucky and the bride can afford it, you'll be receiving a new dress.

If you're buying off-the-rack, as most bridesmaids do, take the dress to a tailor you trust and have it altered so it fits you perfectly. You'll feel better and look more confident, no matter the style or color. Heed this edict from Oscar-winning costume designer Edith Head: "A dress should be tight enough to show you're a woman and loose enough to show you're a lady."

Uniformity

It's very likely that no matter how lovely the bridesmaid dress the bride picks, you'll still feel like you did when you wore a uniform in grade school. The bride can also have guidelines on shoes—color and heel height—and other accessories. This list will help you on your shopping expeditions to complete your bridesmaid look.

MATCHING SHOES

Find out if the bride has a preference for style and color. One style may be more flattering for your body type than another when wearing the dress. If you have a choice, try on a pump, a sling-back, a ballet flat, a kitten heel, a sandal, or a peep toe in the weeks before the wedding. Choosing the shoe style that suits you best, even in a required color, can make the assigned costume feel more personal and to your taste. We recommend zappos.com and dsw.com as places to start your shoe hunt.

Searching in vain for the shade the bride has her heart set on? A good shoe-repair shop can do a great dye job on a white shoe. There are also online retailers that specialize in selling shoes that can be dyed for any occasion (dyeableshoestore.com even carries

dyeable vegan shoes). Other online retailers carry an extensive selection of wedding shoes. Keep in mind that the dyeing process
can shrink shoes. Order a half size larger than you would normally
wear. If the dyed shoes feel too roomy or slip on your heel, you can
add pads or foot liners. This will ensure a more comfortable fit
than a too-tight shoe.

Try on shoes in the afternoon when your feet are typically a
half size larger than they are in the morning. It might make sense
to take along an extra pair to the reception that look good with the
dress but are more conducive to kicking up your heels. After
the obligatory photos and post ceremony, the bride probably won't
mind if you slip on a more comfortable pair of shoes. Reese With-
erspoon wore cowboy boots at her second wedding reception!

WRAPS/CARDIGANS/SHAWLS

You'll want a color-coordinated wrap if it's a cooler season or the
air-conditioning is blasting. A famous real estate tycoon's mistress-
turned-second-wife was witnessed warming her nipples under a
hand dryer in a ladies' room at a reception so they'd be less noticeable under her silk dress. Don't be the star of a similar anecdote.
Which leads us to . . .

UNDERGARMENTS

Bridesmaids need to be as invested in their undergarments as
the bride is in hers. Keep in mind you'll be on display all day, and

who knows what romance the night may bring. You'll need the right brassiere, so take the bridesmaid's dress to a good lingerie shop and ask the saleswoman to help you choose the right bra to wear under it. Stray straps or itchy lace are a nuisance you'll want to avoid on the day you want to keep calm, collected, and smiling. You don't want to realize the morning of the wedding that your only clean bra is your gym bra. Do we have to even mention visible panty lines (VPL)? Treat yourself to a pretty matching thong or underwear that won't broadcast itself underneath a sheer jersey dress. (Keep in mind that your underwear might not appear visible to you, but a photographer's flash can work like an X-ray machine. Just ask Alexandra Kerry what she wishes she could have done differently at the 2004 Cannes Film Festival.)

BAG

A clutch for the reception is a must. While silk or satin is stunning, consider practicality. You may want to set the clutch down on your assigned table when you dance, so don't splurge on this accessory. A tipsy guest may spill a glass of wine on it or pick up the wrong bag on her way home at the end of the evening. You'll want it large enough to hold a phone, a c-note, a credit card, and a condom.

JEWELRY

Some brides present their bridesmaids with a gift to wear for the ceremony, such as a necklace or earrings. While you shouldn't ask,

It's in the Details

Ask the bride in advance about the hairstyle, makeup, and nail color she'd like the bridesmaids to wear for the ceremony. Again, if the bride is flexible, these are subtle ways that you can feel more "yourself" within the parameters of the look the bride wants for her wedding party. That doesn't mean you should show up with a semi-shaved pink hairstyle if you've always had flowing blond tresses! While the bride shouldn't dictate your grooming, it's reasonable for her to expect that you won't tattoo your face a la Mike Tyson before you appear in her wedding photos.

"Hey, are you going to give us some bling to wear on the big day?"—you might ask if the bride has a preference about the jewelry you're going to wear with your outfit. Of course, if you are married or engaged, you're going to wear your ring. But maybe you typically wear a leather cuff with a watch that's going to look too heavy with a silk cocktail dress. Or you like gold hoop earrings, and the bride has been envisioning pearl studs for her bridesmaids. Ask, because the bride may not think of this with all the other details she has to focus on, and the jewelry will be noticeable in the wedding photos.

Beauty and the Bridesmaid

Beauty is pain.

—DOROTHY STEIN (Sarah's grandmother)

It still takes work to look your best when you're dolled up in a gorgeous dress you hand-selected to flaunt your best assets, and you have face-enhancing makeup and a hairstyle of your own choosing. It is obviously more challenging to look fabulous when all of these decisions are completely out of your hands. An unflatteringly cut dress in a color that makes you look jaundiced can present even the most natural beauty with new challenges.

You might even feel like the bride wants you to look like crap. While, in fact, there are stories of brides who have confessed to choosing poorly cut dresses and ridiculous hairdos on their bridesmaids in an effort to ensure the maids don't outshine them on their big day, a bride who is a true friend will want you to look and feel your best. She just won't have time to show you how. That's where we come in.

We've spoken to some of Hollywood's top stylists and makeup artists and gotten some of their best tips and advice on how to make the most of your assets with whatever tulle-embellished cards you've been dealt. That way you'll look your absolute best when you hit that red—we mean white—carpet.

As noted, most likely the bride has already picked out what you're going to wear, and if she hasn't, you can bet she'll be doing it soon and you most likely will hate it. She'll say something like, "It's such a great dress—all you have to do is _____ it (insert: hem, dye, mutilate, shred . . .) and you can wear it again!" Please note: Unless it's black, you will never wear it again. Sorry, Vera Wang.

You could get to pick out any dress in any length in the pink, green, eggplant, or azure blue that matches the table linens, but chances are, unless it's black, EVERY time you put that dress on, you're going to think you look like a bridesmaid—and that's because you probably do. So get over it and move on.

Here's the deal. Being part of a wedding is essentially like being part of a Broadway show. You're a player in that show and part of an overall picture. Brides are looking for a consistent aesthetic, and showcasing your individual beauty is not what the bride is trying to do, even if you are her Bestie. Your job as a bridesmaid is to be part of that overall picture, the vignette, a stage set. How you look as an individual doesn't really matter. I know, I know, that's horrible! It's a travesty! Well, it's the truth. And let us be the first to tell you that those bright colors you don't feel suit your skin tone are going to look great in (airbrushed) photos (so you won't look as jaundiced). At least, they'll look great in the bride's opinion, which is all that really matters anyway. After all, it's not like you're going to keep a framed wedding photo from your friend's wedding on display in your own home.

When you're at a wedding, the guests don't see you as an individual. You're painting a picture and creating an ambience—from the top of your bun to the bottom of your satin shoe. Your dress is part of a bigger scheme, as are you, and if you want any peace at all, you need to embrace that you will be beautiful not in standing out but rather in doing your part to blend in.

So what do you do to make yourself feel or look good when you're wearing a kelly green floor-length gown that makes you look like the Little Mermaid? Well, we can't work miracles. But if the bride lets you have any say in your accessories, shoes, hair, and/or makeup, we can help work with the cards you've been dealt, and help you look, well, like yourself and feel your very best.

MAKEUP AND HAIR

"Think of yourself as a model," says LA–based celebrity makeup artist Daniel McFadden. "You don't get to pick what goes on you. The bride has an overall 'theme' and your job is to work it!"

Of course, if you do choose how you want your own hair and makeup, there are things you should take into consideration:

- Just because you're wearing a green dress doesn't mean you need green shadow, green liner, green mascara, and green eyebrows—unless of course, the theme is *The Wizard of Oz*. Consider neutral and complementary colors. You can always accent your eyes with a little bit of green liner if you want a dash of color. Consult with the bride to see if she has any ideas for your makeup. She'll probably want all of you in similar complementary shades so that as a unit you'll look . . . united.

- If the bride doesn't have in mind a specific look for her brides-maids, and color of the dress is hideous, go with neutral makeup. Don't try so hard to coordinate with it.

- If you don't usually wear makeup, make your friend's wedding your one exception. We suggest stopping by a department store or Sephora a week or two beforehand and getting your makeup done. If you want to avoid looking too made-up, guide the makeup artist with some looks you've seen and think might work on you. Bring a picture from a magazine of a model or an actress with makeup you like, but be sure she has the same natural coloring as you. Even if that picture of Mila Kunis you found is "perfection!" and "just what you want!" if you're a blonde Swede the makeup they used on her in the photo shoot just isn't going to work on you.

- Focus on making your skin look flawless: Clear skin is always beautiful, and you can consider getting a facial two weeks (not closer) to the wedding for a little extra glow.

- Don't neglect your eyebrows: Bushy eyebrows (or worse, skinny penciled eyebrows) don't look pretty. Great brows help frame your face.

- White teeth: You don't need to undergo an expensive teeth-whitening process to have a bright smile for the wedding. Start using a whitener at least a month before the wedding to help pump it up.

- Is the wedding at the Biltmore (i.e., formal) or is it a beach wedding in Malibu (i.c., casual). If it's a formal wedding, those flip-flops and wavy hair might look out of place. Conversely, bright red lipstick and a complicated updo just don't look at home on the shore. Consider the setting, and consult any magazines or websites for ideas on hairdos and looks that might work best.

- If you think you'll want an updo, many salons suggest you don't wash your hair the morning of the wedding. Have the bride check in with the salon to find out what's preferred.

The most important thing to remember is that the wedding is a Broadway play, and you're one of the actors. So even if it's not your personal preference to wear orange chiffon or buttercup, you'll be beautiful by being a really good friend, blending in, and doing your part in helping to create the setting for the wedding. Just be sure to wear a button-down to the salon so that you don't risk ruining your updo or have to take scissors to your favorite top.

DAY-OF BEAUTY TIPS

Here are some items you or the MOH should have available to make sure you and the rest of the bridal party look your best on the wedding day:

- A steamer—to get out any wrinkles
- A lint roller

- Double-sided tape
- Backless adhesive bras—more for girls up through size C or D
- Bobby pins
- Safety pins
- Band-Aids
- Nipple coverage/pasties
- Static guard

7

The Bridal Shower

The bridal shower is the most recognized and significant of the bridesmaid's responsibilities. The tradition is believed to date back several centuries to Holland, where a young woman was deprived of her customary dowry because her father disapproved of her marriage to a struggling miller. Supportive friends and villagers "showered" her with gifts for her new household. Then, as now, the shower gifts are intended to give the new bride the household items and creature comforts she and the groom will need to set up their home.

Typically, the bridal shower is held at least one month before the wedding, on a Saturday or Sunday, in the late morning or afternoon. But don't feel limited to throwing a shower a month beforehand nor obligated to throw one during the early part of the day. If you're throwing a shower with a more modern theme or activity, such as a wine-tasting class, evening makes more sense. The maid of honor is the executive decision maker but discusses ideas and splits the cost with the other bridesmaids, whether it's held at a restaurant, a private home, or another location. It's not appropriate to ask the bride's or groom's relatives to contribute financially, but if the offer is made, don't hesitate to accept gratefully.

It is not uncommon for more than one shower to be held for the bride, especially if she has extended family and grew up in a different town from where she now lives and works. The bridesmaids are not expected to attend each shower thrown in the bride's honor. If and when possible, however, the maid of honor should try to plan a shower for a weekend that out-of-town guests, especially those out-of-town bridesmaids, can attend. Check with the bride about shower dates that would work best for her. Also consult the bride and/or her mother about the guest list so nobody who is attending the wedding is inadvertently left off the invitation list(s).

Some brides are happier if they know at least some of the details of the shower, and some brides enjoy a surprise. Take into consideration the bride's personality and possible expectations of what her shower should be: If she listens to Mozart and is planning a waltz for her first dance with the groom at the reception, a local barbecue joint may not be her preferred location. If she's on a bowling team and her fridge is stocked with energy drinks, a garden tea party might leave her underwhelmed. Brainstorm ideas for themes with the other bridesmaids, based on your shared history with the bride. What have been some of her favorite trips or happiest memories or accomplishments so far? If the bride is using Pinterest, look for clues there as to what kind of shower she'd like, and share ideas about themes and a color palette with the other bridesmaids. Finally, keep your lips sealed on the budget and organizational details, even if the bride asks; she has enough on her mind planning for the wedding and honeymoon. Planning the shower and making it look effortless is one of the essential responsibilities of the bridesmaids.

Whatever the theme of the shower, expect to serve refreshments and a light meal, such as spinach quiche, fruit salad, and some desserts. You'll want to allow time for guests to socialize. And perhaps to make it easy for guests, the women can take turns sharing stories of the first time they met the bride. You'll want to break for lunch or encourage people to eat before the bride starts unwrapping her gifts, because once she's on her throne and unwrapping presents, the attention should be fully on her and not on balancing your salad plate and glass of prosecco. Finally, you'll want to play some games.

Let the Shower Planning Begin

Confab with other bridesmaids on what sort of shower you'd like to throw in the bride's honor. First, you'll have to agree on a date, which has been preapproved by the bride. Next, set a budget. Third, select a venue and compile the guest list based on what the venue can accommodate. Once you have the guest list, a few months before the shower, choose or design creative invitations that either tie in to your theme or reflect the bride's aesthetic. You'll want to mail these out five to six weeks before the shower. Be sure to include the bride's registry(ies) on the invitation, or indicate the type of gift people should bring. You should have invitees RSVP three to four weeks prior to the shower.

When you have a general idea of who will be coming, you and your fellow bridesmaids can start on the following a month beforehand:

Plan a menu
Select party favors
Outline games that will be played
Decide whether to pool resources to buy one big gift for the
    bride or to individually purchase gifts (more to open!)
Make a playlist and be sure to include the bride's favorite
    tunes

Here's where we think it makes sense to divide and conquer when it comes to these tasks. Have Party Girl Bridesmaid focus on the games, and maybe Type-A Bridesmaid can come up with the perfect soundtrack for the shower.

DURING THE SHOWER

At least two bridesmaids at each shower should record the gifts the bride receives so that it's a breeze for her to write thank-you notes later. We suggest two because that way you both can enjoy the fun and exclaim over gifts without the worry of missing recording an item. In the whirlwind of excitement, it's easy to forget who gave what. Did college friend Jessica give the cake knife and salad servers, or was her gift the naughty lingerie apron? The details blur, but the bride's attendants help her look good by remembering everyone's contributions to her happiness.

TIMETABLE

Six months before the wedding, start pre-planning. Discuss the basics of the shower with the other bridesmaids and the maid of honor. The maid of honor should spearhead this effort, but don't wait for her to call. If you haven't heard from her at least **four months** before the date of the wedding, contact her. If possible, get together for lunch, dinner, or cocktails and have fun; laughter always generates more creative ideas!

Three months before the shower, purchase invitations (if ordering printed invitations, choose them **four months** before the party). Book a venue and/or reserve rental furniture.

Five to six weeks before the shower, address and mail the invitations.

One month before the shower, book the caterers and order any food you're planning to serve.

Three weeks prior to the shower, get together again or reconnect via Skype with your cohostesses and review plans and confirm responsibilities.

☐ Will someone be the official photographer of the event? Decide whether to give a group gift.

☐ Follow up with any invited guests who have not yet responded.

☐ Order flowers.

☐ Choose your outfit.

Two weeks before the shower:

☐ Confirm location and/or rental furniture and items such as tablecloths and flatware.

☐ Purchase decorations.

☐ Buy a personal gift and a card for the bride.

☐ Purchase group gift for the bride (optional).

☐ Order alcohol and arrange pickup or delivery.

☐ If you have pets, inquire whether any of the bridesmaids have allergies and plan accordingly.

One week before the shower:

☐ Touch base with your cohostesses.

☐ Purchase nonalcoholic beverages.

☐ Cook anything that can be frozen.

- ☐ Stock up on ice.

- ☐ Plan a fun way to arrange scissors, tape, pencils, pens, and notepads.

- ☐ Buy any other necessary supplies for the games.

- ☐ Confirm order and delivery of catered food.

- ☐ Plan for parking; you may want to alert neighbors with a thoughtful note in their mailboxes that a shower will be held between the hours of x and y. They'll be that much more accommodating for the consideration you've shown them.

Two days before the shower:

- ☐ Begin to decorate (if the shower will be in a private home).

- ☐ Shop for main food items.

- ☐ Clean the house!

- ☐ Set out the alcohol that doesn't need to be chilled, and chill proper bottles.

- ☐ Plan the music.

- ☐ Shop for veggies, fruit, and cheeses.

- ☐ Put together your outfit and accessories, and consider getting a manicure and/or pedicure.

The day of the shower:

- ☐ Have catered food delivered at least one hour before the party.

- ☐ Chop veggies and fruit; arrange cheese and crackers and bread platters.

- ☐ Arrange the main dishes.

- ☐ If hosting at your home, remove drugs and snoop-proof your medicine cabinets.

- ☐ If hosting at a restaurant, arrive with enough time to set up decorations and ensure that the menu and drinks you decided on are ready to go.

Bridal Shower Ideas

Choosing a theme can make a party more personal and add charm as well as provide you with a general guideline for decorations and a design for the invitations and games. The bridal shower is also a great way for bridesmaids to help the bride get different design ideas that she won't use for her wedding out of her system. You may want to consult with the bride or check out her Pinterest board to see if there are any ideas or themes she may want to "exorcise." After all, a theme that reflects the couple's interests and tastes will help steer the guests to choosing gifts the couple will actually be able to use.

THEME IDEAS

WISHING WELL (SOMETIMES KNOWN AS THE GADGET SHOWER)
This is a traditional theme for a shower, in which gifts are placed in a receptacle that resembles a wishing well. Let the couple's interests and registry inspire other gift ideas and continue the theme of the party: a big beach blanket covered with beach-related gifts, a wheelbarrow for gardening enthusiasts, or a canoe filled with camping necessities. A smaller basket entwined with flowers can be filled with handwritten wishes (or cards with checks inside to fund a honeymoon) for the couple. You can also build a wishing well and fill it with household items that might be too small or overlooked on their wedding registry if the couple is setting up a first home:

- Meat tenderizer
- Herb/spice rack with herb and spice bottles
- Measuring cups and measuring spoons
- Apple peeler
- Outdoor thermometer
- Ice cream scoop or melon ball scoop
- Rolling pin

AROUND THE CLOCK/ TIME-OF-DAY SHOWER

For this shower theme, each guest is assigned a different time of day and is instructed to bring a gift that might be used at that hour. If you have a lot of guests, break the time into half-hour intervals or duplicate the hours. This provides the guests with a framework within which they can exercise their creativity. One guest might think a massaging showerhead is the perfect gift for 7:00 a.m., and another might choose an alarm clock with a big snooze button. Here are some other examples:

- 7:00 a.m.—Travel alarm clock, yoga mat, workout clothes, gift certificate to a local coffee shop, juicer, bathroom mirror
- 8:00 a.m.—Eggcups, newspaper subscription, breakfast-in-bed tray, coffee mugs
- 9:00 a.m.—Cereal bowls, omelet pan, fruit-of-the-month or croissant subscription, coffeemaker, waffle iron
- 10:00 a.m.—Toaster oven, basket of preserves and honey, iron and ironing board
- 11:00 a.m.— Bread box, linen tablecloth and napkins, spa certificate
- Noon—Picnic basket, glass tumblers, outdoor furniture, gardening tools
- 1:00 p.m.—Artisanal mustards, Zagat/restaurant guides, panini grill for sandwiches
- 2:00 p.m.—Box of chocolates, cookie sheet, pie dish
- 3:00 p.m.—Cozy blanket and pillow (nap time)

- 4:00 p.m.—Teakettle, tea pot, baking sheet for madeleines, dessert plates
- 5:00 p.m.—Martini glasses, universal remote, steak knives
- 6:00 p.m.—One or more settings of china pattern the bride has chosen for her registry
- 7:00 p.m.—Pizza stone, cookbook, pizza cutter, bottles of imported olive oils
- 8:00 p.m.—Red and white wineglasses, flatware, Netflix gift certificate
- 9:00 p.m.—Brandy or port glasses, bath salts, aromatic candles
- 10:00 p.m.—Sleep machine, down pillows, fragrant firewood, cozy pajamas
- 11:00 p.m.—His and her bathrobes, lingerie, sex toys (don't forget batteries)
- Midnight—Popcorn popper, massage oils, eye mask, wax earplugs (if the groom snores)

This theme doesn't necessitate a certain look or feel, so decorate and serve food that you know the bride would appreciate and love.

KITCHEN SHOWER

This might be the theme to go with if the bride enjoys cooking and experimenting in the kitchen. You can update this traditional theme with an *Iron Chef* or *Chopped* twist, and ask guests to bring a gift inspired by their favorite celebrity chef. For example, a fan of Wolfgang Puck could bring a pizza stone and packaged smoked salmon; a Nigella Lawson fan might opt to bring a decadent cake plate and goose fat. (The bride must be a gourmet cook to know what to do with that!) Popular items to get are:

- Dish towels
- Toaster
- Blender
- Trivets
- Fun magnets for the fridge
- Everyday glasses

AROUND-THE-HOUSE SHOWER

Assign your guests a room in the house to inspire their shower gift, and the following line can be added to the invitation: "Please bring a gift for the _____" (kitchen, bathroom, etc.). Since this theme doesn't require a certain aesthetic, you can decorate and serve anything you think the bride might like.

ALICE-IN-WONDERLAND SHOWER OR *DOWNTON ABBEY* TEA

For an Alice-in-Wonderland theme, locate Tim Burton–style mismatched chairs, funky furniture, and lighting. If you don't have a funky teahouse in your area, consider renting teacups and serving pieces from a caterer, buying inexpensive teacups from Goodwill or fishseddy.com, or splurging on a set from MacKenzie-Childs, which has a whimsically madcap look that will stay with the bride. Serve rich desserts and decorate with colors. Gifts don't have to tie directly to teatime and can fall in the general cooking/baking category.

For a *Downton Abbey* theme, note that elegance prevails, and find a place that offers linen tablecloths and napkins. Find vintage teacups and tea services (Lady Grantham's pattern is Herend Chinese Bouquet in Rust), and serve small tea sandwiches and lobster salad.

HONEYMOON SHOWER

Throw a shower that'll give the bride items she can use while walking along the Seine in Paris or on the beach in Saint Lucia or Cancún. Depending on where the bride's travels will take her, you can consider the following:

- Beach towels
- Glamorous sunglasses
- Linen hat
- Silk scarf
- Travel guide for the honeymoon destination (her focus has been on the wedding; she may not even have picked up one of these yet)
- Makeup bag
- Tote bag
- Lingerie bag
- Kindle or Nook
- Backpack (if she's going camping, on a safari, or to the Amazon)

Decorate and serve foods that the bride will encounter and enjoy on her honeymoon.

LINGERIE SHOWER

This theme is a particularly good idea if the bride's lingerie wardrobe consists of racerback bras and full briefs. Gift her with risqué lingerie she most likely wouldn't purchase for herself, such as babydoll negligees and G-strings, teddies, bustiers, and garter belts. Treat her to some extravagant designers like La Perla and Agent Provocateur, or for virginal but luxurious cotton gowns, Celestine. If you can't find a beautiful or racy enough selection locally, try:

bitsoflace.com
agentprovocateur.com
figleaves.com
kikidm.com
laperla.com/en-us/
trashy.com
brooklynfoxlingerie.com
hankypanky.com
pinkgirlvintagelingerie.com
For plus sizes: buciolingerie.com

Decorate using costume jewelry and textured fabrics, and serve chocolate-covered fruits and prosecco.

LINEN SHOWER

Be sure to check the bride's registry, but this is where you can take an idea a little further and shower her with luxurious towels, decadent sheets, and beautiful linen napkins. Consider whether these are the sort of indulgences the bride didn't allow herself to register for and may not have because she's too modest for her own good. Because linens are delicate and indulgent, serve such food as crepes, dosas, soufflés, and decadent desserts.

SEASONAL/TIME-OF-YEAR SHOWER

This theme is exactly what it sounds like, and perfect for the bride who loves to spend time outdoors, whether to go on picnics or hikes. You can pick a season or assign each guest (more than one can be assigned) a month of the year. Decorate using the outdoors, with birch-covered candles and wildflowers. And for fun, serve foods you might eat outside, like hot dogs, hamburgers, and s'mores.

Spring

- His and hers umbrellas
- Birdbath
- Gift certificate to a local nursery
- Tennis or golf lessons
- Tickets to a local baseball team's opening game

Summer

- Badminton set
- Croquet set

- Sprinkler
- Hammock

Fall

- Flower bulbs
- Rake
- Wheelbarrow
- Weekend at a bed-and-breakfast in New England during the peak of foliage season

Winter

- His and her ice skates
- Cashmere throws
- Crock-Pot for making stews
- Bird feeder
- Tickets to a local play or musical

HOBBY SHOWER

If the bride-to-be is a crafting queen, big golfer, or jet-setter, consider throwing her a shower that revolves around her hobby. For this shower, you'll especially want to guide guests on what to bring. Since this theme focuses on the bride's favorite pastime, consider decorating with her favorite color or the wedding colors. Serve one of her favorite foods.

FRENCH COUNTRY SHOWER

This is a great theme for the bride who loves the French countryside. You can serve croque madames (easy and inexpensive to make!) and French pastries. You can decorate with perfume bottles or, better, go to a perfume bar. At a perfume bar soiree, the bride can create the custom fragrance she'll wear for her wedding day.

BREAKFAST AT TIFFANY'S SHOWER

If the bride is always found sporting pearls and big sunglasses, this may be the perfect shower for her. Have guests wear their favorite LBD and supply everyone with fake pearls and big hats. Instead of a game, engage everyone in an activity. Set up a fascinator-making station, where they can take little headbands or combs and glue on fun fixin's. Decorate with costume jewelry and vintage anything. Serve cocktail meatballs and cheese puffs, and make sure the ladies are all sipping from champagne coupe glasses (plastic ones are fine).

FOODIE SHOWER

If the bride is a foodie, consider having a professional chef come and teach a class to attendees. Or arrange to have a cheesemonger give a tutorial and tasting of cow's milk, goat's milk, and sheep's milk cheeses. Gifts can be cheese themed, such as a cheese board and knife set and cheese dome. Or maybe just allow guests to go off the bride's registry.

WINE LOVER SHOWER

If the bride is an oenophile or a budding wine aficionado, bring in a sommelier from a local wineshop or restaurant to do a tasting. Or do your own! Guests can gift the bride a lovely crystal decanter, a wine coaster with an intricate design, or an antique one stamped with the year the bride was born. For fun, use grapes to decorate and be sure to serve carbs that can soak up wine.

SHOWER GAMES AND ACTIVITIES

No matter the theme, there are certain games and activities that can be interspersed throughout the shower for additional fun and entertainment. As with everything related to the wedding, consider whether or not the bride will approve of and enjoy the games and activities you select.

THE BRIDAL GOWN GAME

Hostesses provide multiple rolls of toilet paper. Guests get assigned to groups of four, and each group gets one roll of toilet paper and selects a "model" from the group. They then design a wedding gown and headpiece for her constructed with the toilet paper. No tape or glue allowed! Then present a mock fashion show and the bride selects the winner (see page 130 for suggested prizes).

THE CLOTHESPIN GAME

This one has been around for several generations (ask your grandmothers for game suggestions). When each guest arrives, a clothespin is attached to her sleeve. The guests are instructed *not* to cross their legs during the party. Whoever catches another guest crossing her legs claims the offender's clothespin(s). The goal is to collect as many clothespins as possible.

The Roast

Guests are asked to come prepared with limericks, poetry, or anecdotes about the bride to read aloud at the shower (set a time limit on how long they can be, say, two minutes). This game can cause hurt feelings though, since what one person deems "edgy" humor can actually sting. If the bride is Sarah Silverman or a staff writer for *The Onion* or *Saturday Night Live*, this is the way to go.

The Wedding Night Game

This risqué game was invited by the Mad Men generation. One of the bridesmaids secretly writes exclamations or remarks made by the bride as she opens each gift. After all the gifts have been opened, the remarks are read to the guests as the things she'll say on her wedding night: "What is this?" "Oooh, I've been wanting one like this!"

The Trivia Quiz

Ahead of time a sheet of questions about the couple, the answers to some of which can only be guessed, is prepared, and copies are distributed among the guests. The questions are read aloud by one of the bridesmaids and the bride responds with the correct an-

swers. The guest who answers the most questions accurately wins.
Sample questions:

Where did the bride and groom meet?
What are the middle names of the bride and groom?
What does the bride like best about her fiancé?
What did the couple do on their first date?
What was their first trip together?
What was the name of the groom's childhood pet?
What is the bride's favorite expression?

Of course, the questions can be a lot racier, depending on the guests. We'll leave those to your imagination and discretion!

Prizes are a fun way to provide a little incentive and introduce some friendly competition into a shower game. They are also cute tokens of the shower for the winners, and they don't need to be expensive. So be prepared to have prizes for winners or favors for each guest to take home. Some ideas include small picture frames, sachets, attractive notepads, fragrant soaps, atomizers, bookmarks, small leather journals, luggage tags, potted plants, bud vases, herbal teas, paper coasters.

If none of the bridesmaids feels comfortable having a shower in their home (or if no one has a house or apartment that can accommodate everyone) and the expense of a restaurant or small venue is too daunting, feel free to think outside the box for other fun activities and places. This list offers some ideas of where to shower the bride with love and affection:

The Bowling Shower—Take the shower to the bowling alley!

The Spa Shower—Everyone enjoys manicures and pedicures. Serve mimosas or champagne in (plastic) flutes. If the wedding is just a few days away, advise the bride and other bridesmaids to avoid getting a facial.

The Yoga Shower—As the countdown to the big day begins, help the bride take deep breaths and find inner tranquillity.

The Carnival Shower—Some weddings start to feel like a circus. Get a head start with a colorful tent, boozy snow cones, lots of stripes, and cotton candy.

Itemized Bridal Shower List

Expense	Item	Estimated Cost	Actual Cost
VENUE LOCATION			
FOOD AND DRINK	Food, caterer		
	Appetizers		
	Entrées		
	Dessert		
	Nonalcoholic beverages		
	Alcohol/liquor		
	Linens		
	Decorations		
	Flowers		
	Flatware		
	Servingware		
	Glassware, cups		
	Shower cake		
Food and Drink Subtotal			
INVITATIONS AND POSTAGE			
CAMERA, EXTRA BATTERIES			
PARTY GAMES AND ACCESSORIES			
FAVORS			

Expense	Item	Estimated Cost	Actual Cost
RENTALS (tables, chairs)			
ENTERTAINMENT			
CLEANUP GOODS			
GRATUITIES			
TRAVEL	Airfare to/from bridal shower		
	Hotel accommodations		
GROOMING	Manicure/pedicure* (Use worksheet in Chapter 2 for reference.)		
Bridal Shower Subtotal		Insert total here	
GIFTS			
Gift Subtotal		Insert total here	

*Additional Expense: This is a potential, but discretionary, expense.

8

The Bachelorette
Party/Weekend

Traditionally the bachelorette party (Anglophiles know the Brits call it a hens' night) is held about a month before the wedding. It's usually wise to schedule this pre-wedding soiree no closer than a couple of weeks before the nuptials, because no bride wants to wake up with a hangover on her wedding day, and a radiant bride must have sufficient time to recover from her night of debauchery.

The maid of honor and bridesmaids consult with the bride on the location, activities, and guest list. The cost should be agreed upon beforehand and split evenly among the MOH and brides-maids. (Note: Consult the bride on what she would like, but keep mum on costs.) There's little else that is traditional about the celebration. Anything goes. The goal is to relax, laugh, and reminisce about the bride's life as a single woman and celebrate this next stage of her life in a way that suits her personality and interests. And these days, more and more brides are requesting that their bachelorette party be a bachelorette weekend away. As a result, a well-executed bachelorette party requires ingenuity, planning, organization, and extra funds. It is less formal than the bridal shower, and the bride's mother and FMIL are not invited. So if the bridesmaids decide to combine the bridal shower with an out-of-town bachelorette party, make sure that another shower will be held in which guests who are unavailable to travel or give up an entire weekend can attend.

The guest list should be limited to about a dozen women who are really close to the bride and can be trusted. Who has her back, whether friend or coworker? The invitees should be the loyal, the adventurous, and the trusted. Destination parties and weekend getaways have become popular—this is a great way to whisk the bride away from all the last-minute fuss and the pre-wedding jitters. But try to plan something that will still be affordable for the invitees.

Of course, there may be unanticipated costs that aren't financial (a lost tooth, a shaved head, a tattoo). Those costs should be divided equally, as well, if at all possible.

Some girls like to party hard before they settle down and want the complete *Hangover* experience: drunken carousing, blood pacts on rooftops, and naked, oiled limbs. Pull out a calendar and circle the date with a full moon. What do Carmen Electra, Katy Perry, and Kim Kardashian have in common besides their life stories chronicled on *TMZ*? They all celebrated with strippers at their bachelorette parties in Las Vegas. (And, oh yes, their marriages suffered the same fate, divorce. Hmmm, maybe skip Vegas and aim to create memories closer to home.)

Speaking of creating memories, if you've ever opened your

You can send an actual invite via snail mail, but you may prefer to go the electronic invite route to save on both money and response time. Some great electronic invitation websites are as follows:

paperlesspost.com

punchbowl.com

pingg.com

evite.com

mailbox to withdraw a plain envelope with no return address and found inside a DVD of yourself doing something you'd sort of forgotten about and hoped everyone else had as well, you'll appreciate a new iPhone app called Snapchat. It allows users to send a photo that will disappear in ten seconds or less (keep in mind, another user with fast reflexes could still take a photo of the image before it disappears and share it with the world). And have you heard of TigerText? It's an app that deletes text messages after they've been read and allows you to recall messages before and even after they've been read. Depending on your plan and intentions, you may want to research the latest technology that can afford you more guilt-free freedoms. We've even heard of one MOH who bought each guest a prepaid cell phone that could be tossed away before they went home. But too often there is a witness, someone more careless or with less to lose, who is snapping away without a thought about whether an image might go viral.

Remember the Prince Harry incident: His bare bum and freckled hands cupped over his royal jewels were immortalized in a photo that serves as proof that what happens in Vegas does *not* always stay in Vegas. And he had a security team! If debauchery is on the menu, perhaps a code of honor should be sworn to before the festivities: no texting, no cameras, and no tattling. Or have everyone sign a confidentiality agreement (sample included at the end of the book).

If waking up with livestock or felons is not the bride's cup of tea, there are lots of other ways to blow off steam—either locally or at a fun destination. Here are some popular ideas for a weekend getaway, road trip, and girls' night out:

A Weekend Spa Getaway

If the bridesmaids can afford it, a luxurious weekend at a spa may become an event the bride will want to make an annual tradition. Get the tension rolfed out of you by a muscular stranger who was a Viking in another lifetime. Nibble on organic strawberry-and-arugula salads and luxuriate in eucalyptus steam baths. Learn how to reduce puffiness around eyes with chilled mint leaves and make your skin glow with thyme and fennel seed.

A WEEKEND AT A BEACH OR SKI DESTINATION
Rent a house (check out vrbo.com). Before she takes the big step to Mrs., the bride will appreciate long walks on the beach (not to mention the volleyball players) or will enjoy the fresh air of an alpine mountain while hiking or skiing. Rum is popular in both climates, whether swirled with a pink umbrella or a stick of butter. Lots of ski resorts offer off-season rates, and the towns are just as charming in July as they are in December. Check out Aspen, Crested Butte, Vail in Colorado; take a treetop canopy tour at Whitefish Mountain, Montana; Smugglers' Notch and Stratton Mountain in Vermont; Jackson Hole in Wyoming.

DISCO NIGHT/ROLLER SKATING
Break out the platform shoes for a feverish night grooving to the Bee Gees, the Bay City Rollers, and the Icon of Love, Barry White. Haven't you heard? Gold-chain necklaces and spandex jeans are trendy again. The bride can find Xanadu under a multifaceted mirrored globe and rub up against white satin that has nothing to do with her trousseau.

A CULTURAL FIELD TRIP
The bride adores Seurat; the groom would rather watch paint dry than walk through a museum. Treat her to tickets to a new show at one of the leading museums in a city with other attractions that would make for a fun getaway weekend.

GOLF TRIP

Single bridesmaids are going to like the male/female ratio at a golf resort. And the ladies who don't know how to play can participate in golf clinics to learn the difference between a birdie and a bogey. And all the top golf resorts feature luxurious spas. Check out: the Boulders in Carefree, Arizona; the American Club Resort in Kohler, Wisconsin; the Cloister in Sea Island, Georgia; Pebble Beach Resort in Pebble Beach, California; Bandon Dunes Golf Resort in Bandon, Oregon; the Greenbrier in White Sulphur Springs, West Virginia; Pinehurst Resort, Pinehurst, North Carolina; the Homestead in Hot Springs, Virginia; Four Seasons Resort Lana'i at Manele Bay in Lanai City, Hawaii; the Four Seasons Resort Hualalai on the Big Island, Hawaii.

MUSIC FESTIVAL

Coachella, Bonnaroo, Bumbershoot, Burning Man, Electric Zoo, Lollapalooza—no, these are not new Muppet characters. They are music extravaganzas that will rock your world and provide lots of sideshows. Most take place during the summer.

COWBOY BAR

Go to an authentic one to find real men who line dance. Let your hair down. Leave your skinny jeans home and kick up your boot heels. Feel your heart race as a Blake Shelton look-alike pulls you closer with callused hands. He rustles steers during the day, and his pickup truck is hitched just outside under the magnolia tree. He introduces himself as Tex, and you never ask for a last name.

TIP: Only dance with a cowboy whose hands are bigger than his belt buckle.

DUDE RANCH WEEKEND

You won't run into Billy Crystal, but you will come home with memories of big skies and broad shoulders. And sore thighs.

CRUISE

Remember *The Love Boat*? Something for everyone! Just bring antiseptic wipes and make sure what you pick up isn't gastrointestinal.

WINE TASTING

Many states have gorgeous wineries that offer tours and tastings and gourmet feasts. Don't forget to bring ID if you look young enough to be carded.

PRIVATE ART PARTY

Drinks, drawing, and a nude model. Each guest gets an apron, an easel, and an eyeful when a nude model poses for the group. You'll learn how to sketch and shadow a buttock, which is so more tasteful than screaming at a man to take his clothes off. (http://www .theartfulbachelorette.com)

POKER NIGHT

So that nobody breaks the bank, instead of chips, play with laminated discs that commemorate memorable people or events in the bride's life. The point is to show the bride how well her friends know and love her, a gift that exceeds any monetary value.

Comedy Club
The perfect venue for making the bride blush and some good-hearted ribbing. Call the club in advance to reserve a table, inquire about a group discount, and be sure to request some mother-in-law jokes.

Karaoke
A fun way to get risqué without getting crass. Sing Marvin Gaye's "Let's Get It On" and rock out to AC/DC's "Shook Me All Night Long."

Camping Weekend
Tell ghost stories around the campfire about the bride's former flames. Keep the bride away from any foliage that you don't recognize. And whatever you do, don't burn poison ivy! We know one bridesmaid who spent a weekend gardening, and then burned the weeds she'd gathered. She ended up in the hospital after inhaling poison ivy resin in the smoke. Know your firewood, and steer clear of freshly chopped wood that may have been growing near poison ivy or oak. Don't forget to pack insect repellent.

The Strip Joint
Whether at Chippendales or a less choreographed stage, many women love to drink and shout, "Take it all off!" This could rub a

few bridesmaids the wrong way. Nobody wants to feel like a spoil-sport, but some of us don't define *fun* as a man with a fake tan gyrating and urging us to rub oil on his body. It can also feel awkward to meet people for the first time in an atmosphere of abandon, only to run into them again at the more formal atmosphere of the wedding.

Final advice: You don't need to have a penis-shaped cake to have a blast and get a little (or a lot) racy. Plan transportation in advance if the booze is going to flow, and ask Party Girl Bridesmaid for that name and number of the nearby bail bondsmen. Wear a wig and dark sunglasses. Don't let the bride make out with a man who has a beard, as beard burn can last a few days. Remember: dark under-eye circles must disappear before the photographer shows up, and all bridesmaids must be accounted for. Leave no woman behind. And no evidence.

Use this chart to calculate expenses for the girls' night out.

Itemized Bachelorette Party List

Expense	Item	Estimated Cost	Actual Cost
VENUE(S)/ LOCATION(S)	Spa		
	Restaurant		
	Bar/club/discotheque		
	Other		
Venue/Location Subtotal			
TRAVEL	Airfare to/from destination		
	Bus fare to/from destination		
	Train fare to/from destination		
	Rental car to/from destination		
	Taxi cabs		
	Party bus		
	Tips		
Travel Subtotal			
ACCOMMODATIONS	Hotel		
	Rental		
	Tips for porters/maid		
Accommodations Subtotal			
FOOD AND DRINK	Breakfast(s)/Lunch(es)/ Dinner(s) for bachelorette weekend		
	Snacks for hotel room		

Expense	Item	Estimated Cost	Actual Cost
	Special dessert for bride		
	Nonalcoholic beverages		
	Alcohol/Liquor		
	Other		
Food and Drink Subtotal			
ACTIVITIES AND ENTERTAINMENT	Concert tickets		
	Spa sessions		
	Comedy tickets		
	Karaoke		
	Stripper		
	Other		
	Tips		
Activities and Entertainment Subtotal			
PARTY FAVORS AND ACCESSORIES	Matching bedazzled shirts/ tank tops		
	Wigs		
	Beads		
	Bunny ears		
	Other		
Party Favors and Accessories Subtotal			

Expense	Item	Estimated Cost	Actual Cost
GIFTS FOR THE BRIDE	Bedazzled bride tank top		
	Tiara		
	Penis anything		
	Other		
Gifts Subtotal			
DECORATIONS	Garland/Banner		
	Balloons		
	Flowers		
	Other		
Decorations Subtotal			
BACHELORETTE PARTY SUBTOTAL		Insert total here	
INCIDENTALS			
HOTEL DAMAGES			
PREPAID CELLPHONE			
BAIL			
		Insert total here	

9

The Wedding Rehearsal and the Rehearsal Dinner

They say in life there are no dress rehearsals. Well, they obviously weren't talking about weddings, because the dress rehearsal for a wedding isn't just a run-through; it's a big part of the wedding celebration.

Walking down a fifty-foot-long path isn't usually so daunting for people, but when there is a life-altering event awaiting you at the end of that path, feet stumble, knees buckle, and normally very "on it" people completely forget where they're supposed to be. The wedding rehearsal is the opportunity for all participants in the wedding to learn their places in the procession and perfect their timing, and for the bride and groom to work through those last-minute jitters.

In addition to the actual wedding rehearsal, it is also customary for the bride and groom (traditionally the groom's family) to host a rehearsal dinner. This is a great way to gather the wedding party and out-of-town guests in a more intimate setting and for members of the wedding party to give speeches (because not *everyone* can ramble on at the wedding). It's also a great time to roast the bride and groom.

The Rehearsal

As with any theatrical event, rehearsals are crucial for a successful show. We all know a wedding is one big Broadway extravaganza, boy lead, girl lead, boy meets girl, boy and girl express their love, they kiss, and then they're married. All in about two hours! There's even a big dance number; it's called the processional (right together, left together, right together, left together, stop and turn). The only thing you don't have is understudies (unless there's something going on with an usher or another bridesmaid that you don't know about). Well, the wedding rehearsal is just a dress rehearsal without the expensive costumes. This is your opportunity to iron out all the kinks in the program before the big show. You'll be performing live, and you'll be subject to intense scrutiny. Perform beautifully, and you'll receive rave reviews, maybe even a standing ovation. Stumble, and the reviews will haunt you until the day you die. Without a rehearsal, who knows what kind of mayhem could break out at the wedding: bridesmaids wandering aimlessly around the chuppah or altar, unsure of where to stand, or even worse, vying for better positioning mid-ceremony; ushers racing down the aisle after the ceremony in search of a keg, deserting their assigned bridesmaid in a cloud of rice. The rehearsal gives everyone in the wedding party an opportunity to go through the motions so that on the big day, when the director (aka the minister, rabbi, judge . . . or wedding planner) says, "Places!" all the actors are on their marks.

Traditionally, the rehearsal is done the night before the wedding. The point of the rehearsal is to give the whole bridal party a chance to "rehearse" the ceremony with a mock processional and a quick run-through of the service. The officiant, and any other people participating in the ceremony—honored guests who might be reading a passage during the ceremony, flower children, and so on—meet at the ceremony site to go through the motions. It is possible, particularly if the ceremony will not be in a church or synagogue, that the rehearsal will be just for the wedding party. It is also possible that the bride may choose not to rehearse, which may be all fine and dandy if the wedding will take place on a farm or it's being taped for a reality show and they want it to be as much of a train wreck as it can possibly be. However, if the wedding is expected to be relatively traditional (for example, guests are expected to eat their meal with utensils and will be wearing shoes), try to persuade the bride to have some sort of rehearsal, even if it is really brief.

Weddings consist of three acts: the processional, the ceremony, and the recessional. It's important to know your place in each so that you can concentrate on trying not to trip on the runner instead of wondering what you're supposed to do when you make it to the end of the aisle. During the rehearsal, the wedding party practices the processional and the recessional so that everyone can take note of their positions during "the show." This is your only opportunity to practice your part, so be a good bridesmaid and try to pay attention. Even if the rabbi is surprisingly hot.

THE PROCESSIONAL

The processional, as we know it today, is actually a drastically abbreviated version of the earliest wedding processionals. While in our society the processional refers to the bridal party's walk down the aisle and up to the chuppah or altar, it is a mere vestige of the original processional. In centuries past, whole villages marched through town from the bride's home to either the couple's new home or the town church. Some villages in countries around the world still perform this ritual. But chances are, the whole town isn't invited to the wedding, and the people who are invited—particularly some of the older folk—don't really care to march around town, ruining their good shoes and aggravating their bunions, so it's safe to say that you can probably find your place in one of the standard processional formations listed below.

There are as many different kinds of processionals as there are religions (including atheism), and it's important to know where you stand in each. Here are the most common processionals:

PROTESTANT

In a Protestant procession, the officiant, the groom, and his best man are not a part of the procession. They are already positioned at the end of the aisle by the altar.

First: Ushers

Ushers enter from the back of the church in pairs, by height, from shortest to tallest. If there is an odd number of ushers, the shortest one should go down the aisle first, with the remaining men entering in pairs. Spacing between each pair should be three or four pews.

Second: Bridesmaids

The bridesmaids follow right behind the ushers. If there are fewer than four bridesmaids, they should walk single file. More than four should pair off according to height. While, technically, bridesmaids are not placed in order of importance during the processional, it is traditional that in the case where there are fewer than four, the bridesmaid who had the most responsibilities is at the back of the line—closest to the maid of honor. If the responsibilities were equally shared, the bridesmaids form a line according to height, with the most petite maid in front. Again, if there is an odd number of bridesmaids, the shortest goes first, by herself. If there are junior bridesmaids, they follow the bridesmaids down the aisle, solo, in order of height.

Third: Maid of Honor

The maid of honor follows the bridesmaids or the junior bridesmaids, if there are any. If there is a matron of honor as well, or two maids of honor, or two matrons of honor (whatever!), they can walk down the aisle side-by-side or single file. It's the bride's choice.

Fourth: Ring Bearer and Flower Girl

These young attendants follow the maid of honor. They can walk together or separately. In the case of the latter, the ring bearer goes first and the flower girl immediately precedes the bride. While these young cherubs add charm to any ceremony, you may want to warn the bride about including extremely young children—those under the age of two and a half can be unpredictable. If she's cool with that, great! But we have more than a few stories of rogue eighteen-month-olds; one who went astray searching the guests for a pretzel stick and another who crouched and announced she went "poo poo." If the bride's on board with this kind of spontaneity, she should just be prepared.

Fifth: Bride and Her Father

"Here comes the bride . . ." She is always on the left arm of her father. Supposedly this custom dates to medieval times when the father might have had to draw a sword to protect his daughter until he could deliver her to the groom.

CATHOLIC

A Catholic processional is the same as a Protestant processional, with the option that the ushers may also already be stationed at the end of the aisle, along with the officiant, the groom, and the best man.

JEWISH

At a Jewish wedding, everyone in the wedding party, including the officiant and both the bride's and groom's immediate families, is part of the processional. ("So that nobody should feel left out. Oy!") Although there are variations on the positioning of the bridal party in the Jewish processional, depending on whether the ceremony is Orthodox, Conservative, or Reform, the common processional is as follows:

First: Rabbi

The rabbi is the first to walk down the aisle. If there is a cantor, he walks alongside the rabbi, on his or her right side.

Second: Bride's Grandparents

"Bubbe and Zyde," as the bride may affectionately call them, follow the rabbi. They wear a relieved grin because they worried little Rachel might never find a match in law school.

Third: Groom's Grandparents

This proud couple follows the bride's grandparents. An advantageous position from which Grandma Goldberg can check out Grandma Stein's gown and comment to her husband on the tackiness of wearing beading in the afternoon.

Fourth: Ushers and Bridesmaids

They march in pairs of twos made up of one boy and one girl—like the animals onto Noah's ark. These couples proceed down the aisle together in order of height, from shortest to tallest. Of course, if there are more bridesmaids than ushers, an usher may escort two bridesmaids down the aisle at once. This coed pairing can probably be traced back to a shrewd matchmaker in the shtetl. No self-respecting yenta would ever pass up an opportunity to introduce a nice Jewish boy to a nice Jewish girl.

Fifth: Best Man

The best man walks alone (even if there are two of them).

Sixth: Groom and His Parents

In the Jewish procession, the groom is always escorted by his parents, with the father on his left and the mother on his right. The march down the aisle is easy. It's getting the mother of the groom to let go that gets tricky.

Seventh: Maid of Honor

As in a Christian ceremony, if there are two honor attendants, they can walk either side-by-side or single file,

with the honor attendant who had the most responsibilities marching just before the bride.

Eighth: Ring Bearer
The ring bearer follows the maid of honor and marches
down the aisle solo. Sometimes, if there isn't a cute
child in the bride's or groom's family to fulfill this role,
a beloved pet will be entrusted with this honor. Like a
dog or cat. We've not yet seen a bird or lizard as a ring
bearer, and we hope you don't witness this.

Ninth: Flower Girl
Like the ring bearer, the flower girl marches down the
aisle solo. See the section on Flower Girls under Protestant Processional for our caveats.

Tenth: Bride, Her Father, and Her Mother
Enter, the main attraction. As with the groom, the bride
is escorted by both parents: her father is on the left, her
mother on the right. Why? No doubt because she's always "right."

An alternative processional for a Jewish wedding is that the
ushers walk down the aisle separately from the bridesmaids. When
this processional is used, the ushers enter after both sets of grandparents and before the best man. Note that in Orthodox Jewish
weddings, the procession does not include ushers.

CIVIL CEREMONY

This is where an on-site wedding coordinator can come in handy. Whether the wedding is at a large hotel or a small restaurant, there is a person in charge who will be able to help the couple figure out which type of procession best suits their service and the site.

NOTE ON SAME-SEX WEDDINGS

Every wedding needs a processional—bride or no bride, groom or no groom. And since having both spouses already standing at the end of the aisle is just a big yawn (where's the Broadway show production value in that?), both parties should walk down the aisle—together or separate. The choice as to who goes down first can be mutually agreed upon, just as it should be for a good sex life.

THE CEREMONY

Rehearsing the ceremony is almost as critical as rehearsing the processional. Everyone has an assigned place, and you need to know where that place is (see Chapter 10, "He Does, She Does: The Ceremony," pages 174–175). As we mentioned before, practicing the ceremony gives all the players an opportunity to run through their special part at least once. Everyone will be able to see how the ceremony is going to flow and find their cues to get ready—like when the maid of honor takes the bride's bouquet or the best man hands the groom the bride's ring. Whether you're reading a poem or playing an instrument, there are specifics you'll need to cover at the rehearsal—for instance, "How will my poem get to the lectern? Do I have to carry it?" Or, "How do I lower the microphone for my classical trombone solo?"

As in the processional, each person in the wedding party has a designated position when he or she reaches the end of the aisle. Making neat little formations isn't easy, and when you have to fall into line, you realize the wisdom of the people who suggested that the shortest people be closest in. If the tallest people were there, how could you see over their heads?

The following are the most common formations:

PROTESTANT

Officiant

Maid of honor   Best man

Bride   Groom

Flower girl   Ring bearer

Bridesmaid   Usher

Bridesmaid   Usher

Bridesmaid   Usher

Bridesmaid   Usher

An alternative to this formation is the officiant having his or her back to the guests and the couple, maid of honor, and best man facing outward. The attendants then form a semicircle around them—also facing the guests.

CATHOLIC

Again, the positioning for the Catholic ceremony is identical to that of the Protestant ceremony.

JEWISH

In a Jewish ceremony, the bride, the groom, their parents, the honor attendants (best man/MOH) all stand under the chuppah, or wedding canopy. The ushers and bridesmaids stand around the fringes of the chuppah, forming their own neat little shtetl on the outskirts. The grandparents take a load off in the first row. The following is the standard formation around the chuppah.

Rabbi/Cantor

Groom's father   Bride's father

Groom's mother   Bride's mother

Best man **Groom** **Bride** Maid of honor

Usher   Bridesmaid

Usher Ring bearer Flower girl Bridesmaid
(optional) *(optional)*

Usher   Bridesmaid

Usher   Bridesmaid

Usher   Bridesmaid

NOTE ON SAME-SEX WEDDINGS

Whether the ceremony is Protestant, Catholic, Jewish, or Civil (*Civil* being subjective, particularly if the couple have invited disapproving family), there is a place for everyone at the altar or under the chuppah. Where you are in the procession doesn't matter. Just hope you don't end up behind a drag queen, because nobody will even notice you in your fabulously cut bridesmaid dress that you most likely *will* want to wear again. (Isaac Mizrahi and Michael Kors both married their partners; if asked to serve as a bridesmaid for a renowned designer, there will be no anxieties about the bridesmaid dress.)

THE RECESSIONAL

You know the old saying: "What goes up, must come down." Well, once everyone has exchanged their "I do's," you want to make a beeline to the party, right? *Wait!* Not so fast. You still have to perform your duties in the receiving line first. Consult this list to find your place so you can do your job and get on to the celebration:

PROTESTANT

First: The Happy Couple
> The groom is on the left, the bride, physically (and metaphorically), always right.

Second: The Ring Bearer and the Flower Girl
> The flower girl should be on the ring bearer's right.

Third: The Maid of Honor and the Best Man
> The maid of honor is on the best man's right side.

Fourth: The First of the Bridesmaids and the Ushers

The bridesmaid and usher closest to the center aisle are the first to leave. The bridesmaid will be on the usher's right (if there are more bridesmaids than ushers, an usher can escort two bridesmaids at a time).

Fifth: Remaining Bridesmaids and Ushers

After the recessional, the maid of honor joins the bride, the groom, the best man, and the officiant in the signing of the marriage certificate, and then, finally, you're off to the reception!

CATHOLIC

Once again, this follows the same order as the Protestant recessional.

JEWISH

In a Jewish recessional, the order is as follows, with the female always on the left.

First: The Happy Couple

Second: The Bride's Parents

Third: The Groom's Parents

Fourth: The Ring Bearer and the Flower Girl

Fifth: The Maid of Honor and the Best Man

Sixth: The Bridesmaids and Ushers
The bridesmaid and usher closest to the center aisle are the first to leave. The others pair up and filter out behind them.

Seventh: The Rabbi and the Cantor
The cantor is on the rabbi's left, even if the rabbi is a woman and the cantor is a man.

See? Everybody has a place in the wedding. Rehearsing the ceremony, processional, and recessional gives the entire party a chance to familiarize themselves with the traditional as well as the more unique or personalized aspects of the ceremony. Remember, a confident bridesmaid is a happy, smiling bridesmaid.

The Rehearsal Dinner

The rehearsal dinner follows the rehearsal. The groom's parents usually host this event, but it can be given by anyone from the bride's side or even just a close friend. The dinner can be just for the wedding party, or it may be opened up to all out-of-town guests as a way to make a special effort to spend a little extra time with them and thank them for going the extra mile (or miles) to be at the wedding.

In a Christian ceremony, the groom's parents are not part of the processional or recessional, and as such, it is not necessary for them to participate in the wedding rehearsal itself, but they are always included in the rehearsal dinner.

If the bride opts not to host a bridesmaid luncheon, or the bridesmaids don't organize it themselves, the bride will give her attendants a thank-you gift at the rehearsal dinner. This is a token of her appreciation for all of your hard work planning the showers, dealing with dresses, and generally helping out and lending your support throughout the engagement.

More important, the rehearsal dinner not only provides a meal for the tired souls who are exhausted from rehearsing for the big event and are just waiting for it all to be over, but it's also an opportunity for the bridal party and close family to toast (and roast) the bride and groom in a more intimate setting.

As an engaging way to warm everyone up for the wedding, present a montage of the bride and groom growing up or hand out a fun questionnaire about the couple.

Basically, the rehearsal dinner is the perfect forum for sharing intimate and personal memories of the bride and/or groom with the people closest to them. Just try to be conscious that the bride's parents are there and may not appreciate the story about how Stephanie's diaphragm ended up in the Tupperware drawer.

10

At the Wedding!

The shower was fabulous, the bachelorette party was a bash, and the rehearsal went off without a hitch (a real one, at least). You've opened your beautiful gift from the bride and are pleased with your work as a bridesmaid over the past engagement period. With the help of a little melatonin (or Valium?), you've gotten a great night's sleep, and you've awakened with a blemish-free face. You've been preparing for this day for months, and from the confines of your toasty covers, you're feeling in control and confident. Yes indeed, this whole bridesmaid thing just went swimmingly!

Well, pardon the wake-up call, but the real work still lies ahead. Everything up until now was just preparation for opening night, the grand event, the big show. And that curtain is about to rise.

Today you will use all of your carefully honed bridesmaid skills to help you pull off the holy grail of events—a snafu-free wedding day. If you've planned well and prepared thoughtfully, you should make it through this day with very few bumps and bruises (we make no concessions for acts of God.) If you haven't, you still have an opportunity to make up for it. Consult with the MOH as early as possible and get the plan for the day. Check your shared Google calendar and Facebook wedding page. As long as your dress isn't still at the cleaners—and the cleaners is closed—you can still pull it off as Bridesmaid of the Year.

Wedding Day Checklist

- ☐ Bridesmaid toolkit

- ☐ Dress

- ☐ Shoes

- ☐ Two pairs of stockings/pantyhose

- ☐ Directions to the service and reception

- ☐ A Garmin or navigation system in case you lose the directions to the service or reception

- ☐ Invitation

- ☐ Makeup

- ☐ Handbag/clutch

- ☐ Shapewear/underwear

- ☐ Bra/bustier

Superstitions. If the bride writes the names of her unmarried friends on the sole of her shoe before she walks down the aisle, the name that rubs off first will be the next person to get married.

☐ Required headgear

☐ Extra ponytail holder/barrette/hair clips

☐ Your cell phone

☐ Your cell-phone charger (so it doesn't die before you even make it to the nail salon)

☐ Camera (if you want to take better quality pictures than those with your phone)

PRIMPING

Primping with the bride and other bridesmaids is one of the best parts about being in the wedding party. You're all sitting around, chatting, munching on snacks, and sipping champagne while people play with your hair and make you pretty. There's a lot of excitement surrounding a wedding. When a friend's marriage is about to become a reality and you are a member of the wedding party, you're right in the middle of the action. Chances are, you and the bride won't remember much, so make sure you take lots of pictures and video. You never know what will make a great viral YouTube video.

If you're getting your hair done professionally, wear a button-down shirt. One dedicated bridesmaid we know spent a small fortune to have her hair done at the salon alongside the bride. Her hair looked gorgeous. But she was wearing a tight T-shirt and couldn't get it over her head without ruining her coif. Another bridesmaid had to cut the T-shirt off her body. There went another fifty dollars out the window.

SAY "CHEESE"

Formal wedding photographers are the bane of every bridesmaid's existence. You're on your feet, wearing platform heels in soft grass, standing straight in a dress you hate that's too tight, while the photographer asks you to turn this way and that—for what feels like forever—waiting for the guy to finally say, "Okay, now the ushers." Phew.

Professional photos are a prerequisite of almost every wedding. Whether the pictures are taken by the top photographer in town or the bride's second cousin, formal pictures capture everyone looking their best (*best* being subjective, depending on the chosen bridesmaid dresses) and providing the bride and groom with keepsake memories of their big day.

While the bride will most likely have given the photographer a list of photos she wants to have taken (she and the groom, the parents, the ushers with the bridesmaids, etc.), ask for a photo alone with the bride and make sure she gets a picture of her alone with each of her attendants. It's such a great picture to have, and it's possible in the flurry of activity she forgot to specifically request these. She'll be grateful you reminded her.

Whatever you do, don't go directly to the photographer and start requesting pictures of you and your boyfriend. That's what your own camera is for. He or she is hired by the bride and groom and is there to capture their big day, not your good time. If you start insisting on certain photos, you might detract from what the bride and groom really want. If there is a photo you really want taken, there's plenty of time at the reception to jump in front of the photographer's lens.

TRIPPING DOWN THE AISLE: THE PROCESSION

You've already practiced your march, and you know just where to stand in the lineup. All that's left to do is focus on the end of the aisle, smile, and try not to fall down. In case there is no wedding organizer there telling you what to do, here are a few hints for marching gracefully down the aisle:

- For a Christian processional, leave three or four pews between you and the pair in front of you.
- For a Jewish processional, leave half the length of the aisle.

- Don't hum.
- Don't text.
- Don't Instagram, Snapchat, or update your Facebook status.
- Don't drag your feet.
- Don't swing your bouquet or carry it in one hand like a clutch. Hold it upright with two hands.
- Don't bite your lips.
- Don't drag your partner.
- Don't make small talk with your designated usher—even if he is really dashing and witty. You have plenty of time for that at the reception.

HE DOES, SHE DOES: THE CEREMONY

Okay. You've gracefully maneuvered your way down the aisle incident-free, you've all formed a perfect V shape, and a roomful of strangers are now staring at you. You're important. You're somebody. People like you! They really like you! And you want it to stay that way. At least for the wedding. These tips are designed to help you maintain that façade of poise:

- Don't chat with your neighbor—even if you are DYING to tell her you left the rehearsal dinner with the cute waiter.
- Don't sniff or fiddle with your flowers.
- If you have to blow your nose, do so discreetly. Hide a tissue in your hand under the bouquets before you head down the aisle. FYI, dabbing is better than blowing.

- Don't roll your eyes if the groom stumbles over his vows; don't raise a brow if he pauses before saying, "I do."
- Don't clear your throat—especially when the officiant asks if anyone objects to the union.
- Do try to look interested in the ceremony. Or inspired. Or just serene.

WHAT GOES UP, MUST COME DOWN:
THE RECESSIONAL

Finally, on to the reception! WOOT! WOOTs, HAH-LAHs, and Tebowing are all allowed—right *after* you complete your walk back down the aisle. Try not to turn your stately promenade into a mad dash to the punch bowl.

THE RECEIVING LINE

As guests begin to filter out of the church/temple/ceremony and/ or in to the reception, most likely you'll be a part of the receiving line. The order goes like this:

- First: Bride's mother
- Second: Bride's father (optional)
- Third: Groom's mother
- Fourth: Groom's father (optional. No, we don't know why. Maybe the fathers are off smoking stogies?)
- Fifth: Bride
- Sixth: Groom

- Seventh: Maid of honor
- Eighth: Bridesmaids, in any order they choose.

Groomsmen do not typically participate in the receiving line.

THE PARTY

Once the guests have been greeted and had the opportunity to hug the moms and kiss the bride, it's time to party!

Finally, the guests get to celebrate with the newlyweds, you can mingle to your heart's content, and you can all dance till you drop.

If you haven't been to a wedding reception before, it pretty much goes like this:

- The bride and groom are introduced to the crowd.
- The new couple dances first.
- The parents and bridal party join the couple on the dance floor.
- Everyone joins the bridal party on the dance floor.
- Everyone sits down for the first course or salad (if a buffet is served, people begin to eat).
- There's more dancing.
- The main course is served (if it's a buffet, people continue to eat).
- There's still more dancing.
- The bride dances with her father.
- The groom dances with his mother.

- The dancing gets looser and more creative (alcohol is flowing).
- The bride and groom cut the cake.
- Dessert is served (if it's a buffet, grazing continues).
- There's more dancing and drinking, and aperitifs are served.
- The bride tosses her bouquet.
- The groom tosses the bride's garter.
- The best man tosses his cookies.
- The man who catches the garter puts it on the leg of the woman who caught the bouquet. (They get it on in the coat room.) If you notice the woman who caught the bouquet looks uneasy about a stranger groping his way up her leg (and her date appears angry), quickly pull the bride aside and suggest she announce that she'd like to keep the garter belt after all. In fact, it's a good idea to suggest a Plan B to the bride before the reception, in case of a scenario like this.
- The reception comes to a close and the newlyweds are Tahiti-bound!

It's perfectly okay to Gangnam, Harlem Shake, Electric Slide (or enthusiastically experiment with whatever the latest dance craze), and imbibe copiously. (MOH, remember that you may want to wait until after your speech to really hit the sauce.) You can even flirt with the sax player. Just don't forget that, as a bridesmaid, you're still on duty and have an obligation to the bride. Periodically check in with her and see if she needs you for anything. Make sure she gets something to eat. Chances are she'll spend very little time at her table, and her food may get whisked away before she can even nibble at it. Check her makeup to be sure it's holding up, and help her make a bathroom run, if necessary. While you'll be satisfying the requirements of a bridesmaid, you'll also be fulfilling your most important duty of all: to have a really great time. The bride's spirits will be lifted that much more, knowing her wedding has been a success and her friends and loved ones are enjoying themselves.

TO DATE OR NOT TO DATE

Chances are, the issue of whether or not you can or should bring a date to the wedding will arise at some point before you get to the wedding day. For some bridesmaids, this can be a sensitive and important matter. What if you have a significant other or partner, and you want that person to attend the wedding as your date?

Bear in mind that it is not necessarily your right as a bridal party member to invite a guest. Guest lists are carefully compiled with a very sharp eye toward the bottom line; relationships are weighed against the cost per head quoted to the bride and groom by the caterers. If you are not invited with a guest, it isn't because the bride disapproves of your boyfriend (or girlfriend), or at least that shouldn't be the reason. It's more likely that the budget is strained or the reception hall can only hold so many people, and the guest list must be limited. Guest lists are like tiered wedding cakes; intimate family and closest friends are on the top tier, and extended family and acquaintances are at the bottom. Sounds simple, right? But think about how the bride's second cousin Trisha will feel if second cousin Lisa is invited, and she isn't. The point is that people are invited in groups. If one person from the group is omitted, then people from that same group are offended to discover that people on the same tier are invited. This applies to boyfriends and significant others as well. The bride and groom can't invite one person with a guest and then tell another guest in that same tier that he or she cannot bring a date.

From your perspective, it's "just one more person." But it's not. There are probably ten other people who would like to bring dates. Ten people is the equivalent of an additional sixty-inch table. For a moderate-sized wedding of 100–150 guests, today the line is typically drawn at engaged couples or live-in partners. Smaller weddings may preclude all guests except spouses. Larger weddings with bigger budgets can allow for guests to bring a blind date if they want. If you feel really strongly about having your significant other by your side at the wedding, it is completely acceptable to ask the bride if you may bring them as a date, but be clear that you understand her dilemma, and be ready to accept a heartfelt, "Sorry, but no."

If the bride agrees, you have another potential problem on your hands. You are, after all, on duty. An attendant being at somebody's beck and call doesn't always make for the best date. Often a date must be brushed aside because of bridesmaid duties, and he (or she) may not be able to sit with you at dinner, because you're at the wedding party table. Your date will be in limbo during formal pictures, at the bridal party dance, and fairly often during the evening when you're called upon for impromptu photos. For more established relationships, this isn't a problem, not if your date is independent. But if you want to bring somebody who is relatively new to your life and hasn't met your friends (we know of a bridesmaid who had a first date at a wedding—it didn't last), you may have bitten off more than you can chew. If you are considering bringing a date to the wedding, take the following quiz; answer with yes or no to determine whether you're better off attending solo:

	Yes	No
I have known my date for more than twenty-four hours.	___	___
My date knows my bra size.	___	___
My date has met the bride and/or groom.	___	___
My date is friendly with the bride and/or groom.	___	___
My date knows other people who will be at the wedding.	___	___
My date has seen me naked. On purpose.	___	___
I have a pet name for my date.	___	___
I have a pet name for a very special part of my date.	___	___

If you responded yes to more than five of these statements, you're close enough to your date to know whether she or he will have fun at the wedding, regardless of how much time you spend with them. If you responded no to more than five, it's probably better to go solo. If you've answered no to all of the questions, you're not actually in a relationship at all. You'll have more luck with that sax player.

For a single bridesmaid, a wedding is a great place to meet people. You're in the limelight, you're beautifully coiffed (we hope), and people are watching you shake your groove thang on the dance floor. Moreover, we've never heard a story about somebody being rude to a bridesmaid at a wedding (that's up there with cursing at a nun). So use your elevated status to ask the cute guy at the bar to dance. It's easier to be bold when you're wearing a brightly colored dress. Take advantage of your position, and don't forget to add pictures to those contacts you put in your phone. The next day you many not remember the faces that go with the names.

CATCHING THE BOUQUET

The throwing of the bridal bouquet is one of the most common reception traditions, and there are several theories as to where the custom originated. One belief stems from early England, when it was thought that the bride was endowed with the power to transmit good luck to another person. People at the wedding tried to tear away bits of clothing and snatch her flowers and headpiece. In self-defense, she would throw her bouquet to the grabby crowd. In fourteenth-century France, throwing your bouquet was considered more demure than tossing your undergarments (garter). Either way, the general belief was that the single woman who caught the bouquet would be the next to marry.

Unfortunately, for every winner, there are numerous losers. For one woman to walk away triumphantly from the toss, the rest of the single women have to return to their seats as losers. Due to advances of feminism, many brides have chosen to forgo this tradition, and grateful women with poor catching skills have heaved a collective sigh of relief.

However, many brides like to stick with tradition and feel compelled to include this ceremonial toss in their reception schedule. As a bridesmaid, it's important to note that if you are single, you must participate. You don't have to make a dive for the daisies, but you should at least put your arms in the air. While it's difficult to reconcile subscribing to feminist values and stretching for a Prince Charming talisman, this is more about being a good sport. Can't imagine Hillary Clinton or Gloria Steinem leaping for the bouquet? If you really just can't muster the enthusiasm to participate, hide in the bathroom until it's over.

TOASTING TIPS

If you are the maid/matron of honor (or one of the maids/matrons of honor), you will be expected to give a speech. Here are ideas for speech material and a public-speaking tip:

- Childhood and school memories are always touching source material.
- Avoid bringing up the bride's previous boyfriends or past sexual escapades.
- Simple congratulations are perfectly acceptable.
- Speak up so everyone in the cheap seats can hear you.

Superstition: Something old, something new, something borrowed, something blue. This superstition is perhaps the most widely recognized of bridal mythology. The *old* represents good luck from the bride's single life being carried into her married life. The *new* symbolizes her new life with her husband. *Borrowed* is the tie that binds her to friends and community. And *blue* is for purity and fidelity.

11

The Party's Over

It's late Sunday night, you've just gotten home from the airport. You stumble inside with your luggage and consider whether it's too late to defrost the Lean Cuisine lasagna for dinner. You realize you stripped the sheets off your bed before the wedding trip, and now they're sitting, damp and mildewy-smelling, in the washer. It occurs to you that you're supposed to prepare a report for an early-morning meeting at the office tomorrow. You reflect on the fact that the newlyweds are landing in St. Barts right now and may be enjoying a tropical drink as you floss your teeth. It's a little depressing, isn't it? The party's over, and you've got a wrinkled chartreuse dress and credit card bills to think about. Are you going to grow old in your one-bedroom apartment with just your cat for company? Stop right there!

1. Open a can of salted nuts (you need quick protein).
2. Fill a tall glass with water, ice, and a wedge of lime or orange.

3. Draw a bubble bath.

4. Turn up some Miranda Lambert or Ella Fitzgerald.

5. Snack in the tub with a good paperback or magazine.

You must hydrate, nourish, and replenish yourself.

You're back at the helm of your own ship, ready to resume your own life's journey. Your first order of business is pampering yourself. Feed yourself, unwind, listen to music while making your bed, climb in, and catch some z's. You've earned them. In fact, we'd like to send you a bouquet of roses and sweet peas as a reminder to stop and smell the roses yourself and appreciate the little things and the beauty you deserve in your own life.

The next morning, you can make a plan to:

1. Recoup the cash you laid out for the presents and the dress. You could list the dress on Ebay or bridesmaidtrade.com. If you and the other bridesmaids list the dresses together, you may sell them faster to another group of bridesmaids. If listing the dress sounds too time consuming, call local consignment shops and find out what percentage of the sale price they'll give you.

2. Donate the dress to a local high school's theater department or to Goodwill or the Salvation Army, and get a charitable donation receipt for your tax return.

3. Use the fabric to make a throw pillow or journal cover. You could embroider the pillow with your own personal joke about the wedding, something you thought repeatedly during the months leading to the wedding and could never say aloud but will now make you chuckle ("When he stood on his wallet, he was tall enough"). Or you can record these thoughts in a journal. Check out stitchedincolor.com for easy directions.

4. Make a kite and take it to the park or beach. Gorgeous guy: "Cool kite! Did you make it?" You: "Yes, can you believe, it was a bridesmaid dress?"

   ◦ thelastpiece.typepad.com/the_last_piece/2009/06/how-to-make-a-kite.html

   ◦ marthastewart.com/271738/making-a-kite (Note: substitute ripstop cloth with the dress fabric)

5. Some bridesmaids like to get together after the wedding for a "trash the dress" photo shoot. If you feel the need for more bonding with your fellow bridesmaids, here's another excuse to get together.

6. Save it for the bride to wear when she's a bridesmaid at your wedding.

12

Just Say No!

The brides-maid must not fail to keep her engage-
ment, except in cases of sickness or death; in the
latter contingency, the bride should be immedi-
ately informed of the fact.

—The Social Mirror

If you had forgotten who the woman was until she rang and asked you to be her bridesmaid, or if you'd hoped never to hear from this individual again and only wish you could forget her, or if you like her but you're going through an incredibly difficult time in your life personally or professionally, you must politely decline the bride's invitation to serve as her bridesmaid. You will save yourself weeks of grinding your teeth and the problems caused by committing to more than you're able to deliver. Better to disappoint the bride now than both her and yourself later. If you must decline the invitation to be a bridesmaid, you should decline the wedding invitation as well. To spare the bride's feelings, it's best to have a previous engagement (imagined or not) that prevents you from being available the weekend of the wedding.

Sample Bridesmaid Confidentiality Agreement Letter

This bridesmaid confidentiality agreement is made between *bridesmaid's name*] (herein referred to as Bridesmaid #__) and [*name*] (herein referred to as the Bride).

The Bridesmaid agrees to the terms of this agreement:

1. The Bridesmaid acknowledges that, in the course of her duties as an attendant for the Bride, the Bridesmaid has, and may in the future, come into the possession of certain confidential information belonging to the Bride, including but not limited to family recipes, lists of former boyfriends, various indiscretions, family skeletons in the closet and costs of wedding.

2. The Bridesmaid hereby covenants and agrees that he or she will at no time during or after her term as an attendant, use for his or her own benefit or the benefit of others, or disclose or divulge to others, any such confidential information.

3. Upon fulfillment of her duties as an attendant, the Bridesmaid will return to the Bride, retaining no copies, all documents relating to the Bride's personal life including, but not limited to, correspondence, photos taken during the bachelorette party, and all other materials and all copies of such materials obtained by the Bridesmaid during the planning of the wedding and celebrations related to the wedding.

4. Violation of this agreement by the Bridesmaid will entitle the Bride to an injunction to prevent such competition or disclosure and will entitle the Bride to other legal remedies, including attorney's fees and costs.

5. This agreement shall be governed by the laws of [*name of the state*].

6. If any part of this agreement is adjudged invalid, illegal, or unenforceable, the remaining parts shall not be affected and shall remain in full force and effect.

7. This agreement shall be binding upon the parties, and upon their heirs, executors, personal representatives, administrators, and assignees. No person shall have a right or cause of action arising out of or resulting from this agreement except those who are parties to it and their successors in interest.

8. This instrument, including any attached exhibits and addenda, constitutes the entire agreement of the parties. No representation or promises have been made except those that are set out in this agreement. This agreement may not be modified except in writing signed by all the parties concerned.

Bride

_____
(Signature)

_____
(Date)

Bridesmaid

_____
(Signature)

_____
(Date)